The
Capitol
Cook Book

૨&

The new Capitol building in Austin at about the time of its dedication in 1888 as photographed by F. Chapman of Austin. Groundbreaking occurred in 1882, the cornerstone was laid in 1885, the building formally dedicated in May, 1888 and finally occupied in September, 1888. Elijah Myers of Detroit was the architect.

The Capitol Cook Book

A facsimile of the
Austin 1899 edition

❧

with added photographs

STATE HOUSE PRESS
Austin, Texas
1995

Library of Congress Cataloging-in-Publication Data

The Capitol cookbook : a facsimile of the original 1899 edition
with added illustrations / new foreword by
Edith Fletcher Williams.
p. cm.
ISBN 1-880510-43-X (hardcover : alk. paper)
ISBN 1-880510-44-8 (pbk.)
1. Cookery, American. 2. Austin (Tex.)—History.
I. Williams, Edith Fletcher.
II. Myers, E.G., Mrs.

TX715.C2412 1995
641.5973—dc20   95-39171

Printed in the United States of America

Cover design by David Timmons

photographs courtesy of
Thomas A. Munnerlyn

STATE HOUSE PRESS
P.O. Box 15247
Austin, Texas 78761

Introduction

In 1899 the Ladies of Albert Sidney Johnston Chapter #105 labored just as long and hard over *The Capitol Cookbook* project as they did in their kitchens, the center of activity in the Victorian homes. Meals were prepared from natural, often home-grown ingredients by or under the supervision of those most interested in the family and in its well-being. The products of this labor were usually enjoyed by several generations of the family; good food made the day's events more palatable and prepared family members for their activities in the world outside. Recipes were family traditions served and shared with pride.

What an honor to participate in the second reprinting of *The Capitol Cookbook*, just in time for the Chapter's 100th birthday in 1996! Albert Sidney Johnston Chapter #105 was named to honor a man who, upon graduation from West Point Military Academy in 1826, served the United States as Regimental Army Commander in the Black Hawk War, the Republic of Texas as Adjutant General and Secretary of War, and the Confederate States of America as General until his untimely death at the Battle of Shiloh in April 1863. General Johnston and his wife had considered Austin their home since 1839 and often remarked on their love for "the hills and the climate." The Ladies who formed the Chapter that bears his name were wives, mothers, sisters, and neighbors of the prominent citizens of Austin and Texas. There is no doubt these Ladies were energetic homemakers first, but also industrious and important participants in their city's and state's development. Since they often lived longer than the men in their families, they were often able

to observe the fruits of their influence upon several generations of citizens both inside and outside the home. It is with
much pride in the early members of the Albert Sidney
Johnston Chapter #105 and the United Daughters of the
Confederacy that we welcome this reprinting to be enjoyed
again today.

—EDITH FLETCHER WILLIAMS
President 1984-1988
Albert Sidney Johnston Chapter #105

President 1988-1990
Texas Division of the
United Daughters of the Confederacy

Dedicated to
The Albert Sidney Johnston Chapter
of the United Daughters
of the Confederacy

TEXAS STATE CAPITOL COST. $3.000.000.

🌀	APRIL					🌀
Sun.	Mon.	Tue.	Wed.	Thu.	Fri.	Sat.
SUN RISES 7—5.35 14—5.24 21—5.14 28—5.04	1	2	3	4	5	6
7	☽8 8:09 A.M.	9	10	11	12	13
14	☺15 4:40 P.M.	16	17	18	19	20
21	☾22 8:18 A.M.	23	24	25	26	27
28	●29 8:27 P.M.	30				

🌀	MAY					🌀
Sun.	Mon.	Tue.	Wed.	Thu.	Fri.	Sat.
SUN RISES 5—4.55 12—4.48 19—4.41 26—4.36			1	2	3	4
5	6	7	☽8 1:04 A.M.	9	10	11
12	13	14	☺15 1:04 A.M.	16	17	18
19	20	☾21 4:15 P.M.	22	23	24	25
26	27	28	●29 11:41 AM	30	31	

IN APRIL OR MAY IS A GOOD TIME FOR THE FARMER TO PURCHASE A BUCKEYE MACHINE.

A calendar page of 1889 featuring the Texas State Capitol. Cost $3,000,000.

*"Cooking is a fine art,
to which you must bring common sense
and judgment."*

... THE ...

CAPITOL COOK BOOK.

———★———

A SELECTION OF

TESTED RECIPES,

.... BY ....

The Ladies of Albert Sidney Johnston Chapter,
Daughters of the Confederacy.

———★———

COMPILED BY

MRS. E. G. MYERS.

AUSTIN, TEXAS.

———★———

AUSTIN, TEXAS:
VON BOECKMANN, SCHUTZE & COMPANY, PRINTERS.
1899.

DEDICATION.

This book is lovingly dedicated to Mrs. R. L. Dabney, one of the mothers of the Confederacy. An old Virginia housewife, who, from fifty years experience, has given the best she has of tested and original recipes to assist in making this book a success. She is proud to help so noble a cause as the Daughters of the Confederacy espouse, and we are proud to have such valuable assistance from so famous a housewife. Her recipes in manuscript, some yellow with age, will always be treasured by

The Compiler,

LOUISE HOLLAND MYERS.

PREFACE.

In placing "The Capitol Cook Book" in the hands of our friends, we ask for it a fair trial. The recipes are not only peculiarly suited to our climate, but come from each household thoroughly tested and highly recommended.

The net proceeds of this book will go to the Albert Sidney Johnston Chapter, Daughters of the Confederacy, for their monument and charity fund.

To the ladies of that chapter, and other friends who have contributed recipes, I desire to express my sincere thanks. Also to the merchants and other business men who have aided so materially with their advertising.

The attention of the Albert Sidney Johnston Chapter is especially called to each and every advertisement, as it is only fair to patronize those who have assisted us so substantially.

Cereals

The dedication of the new Capitol of Texas, which at the time was considered to be one of the largest buildings in the world, made national news. This fanciful drawing appeared in several of the leading publications of the day such as the *Frank Leslie's Illustrated Newspaper*, May 12, 1888.

Inside of the Souvenir Programme of the Grand Dedication Ball in the New State capitol Building, Friday evening, May 18th, 1888. All the board of directors, and the committee members of the ball, reception and floor committees are listed. The programme was printed in full color on both sides and opened to eight by twenty-five inches.

STEPHEN F. AUSTIN

DAVY CROCKETT

Outside of the Souvenir Programme of the Grand Dedication Ball in the New State capitol Building, Friday evening, May 18th, 1888.

Dance Programme for the Grand Dedication Ball, May 18th, 1888. The front cover featured a beautified version of the Goddess of Liberty. The original programme was printed in black and white and opens to seven inches by ten inches.

CEREALS.

~~~~~~~

CORN MEAL MUSH.

Have a kettle of fresh boiling water. Sift one cup of meal into a sauce pan, add 1 teaspoonful of salt, and cold water enough to moisten. Pour in a little hot water, stir till smooth, set on the stove and pour in about a quart of boiling water. Stir constantly till it boils, then cover and set back where it will cook moderately until well done. If necessary, pour in a little more boiling water. Don't scorch.

Serve with milk or butter.

BREAKFAST FOOD.

Put 6 cups of water and 1 teaspoonful of salt into a sauce pan; when it is boiling rapidly, sift in gently 1 cup of Ralston Food, and let boil 5 minutes.

Serve at once with cream or rich milk.

This is a most nutritious cereal.

GRITS.

One cupful of grits.

Four cupfuls of cold water.

Stir till it boils, then cover. Steam till well done, and salt. Should the water boil out before well done, add more boiling water. The longer it cooks the better.

FRIED GRITS.

Slice cold grits, dip in beaten egg and fry a light brown.

RICE.

Rice should be put on in boiling water, and boiled very rapidly for 15 minutes; salt; then set far back on the stove, and steam till done, when it is dry and the grains stand apart.

Milk and butter can be added when done, if preferred.

A NICE WAY TO COOK RICE.

One teacupful of rice boiled, drain carefully, stir in two well-beaten eggs, 1 tablespoonful of grated cheese, ½ a teaspoonful of butter and 1 teaspoonful of salt. Bake a few minutes.

Victoria.   Mrs. R. L. Dabney.

RICE OR GRITS SCRAMBLED WITH EGGS.

Take cold rice or grits and soften with a little warm water, break in 2 or 3 eggs, beat well, salt, and pour in a hot, well greased frying pan. Stir constantly till done. A little grated cheese may be added if convenient.

BAKED HOMINY OR RICE.

Boil 1 cup of hominy or rice until thoroughly done. When cold add 2 eggs, a tablespoonful of butter, salt to taste, a teaspoonful of baking powder and 1 cup of sweet milk. Bake in a hot oven until solid, and serve at once.

Miss Ella Bedell.

RICE, A GOOD SUPPER DISH.

Cook rice well done, add 1 cup of fresh sweet milk, a tablespoonful of butter and a little salt. Let cook a few minutes, remove, and serve with sugar and ground cinnamon or nutmeg.

CROQUETTES.

Mold cold rice or grits in flat cakes, dip in salted egg well beaten, roll in cracker crumbs or flour, and fry a light brown.

GRANITE AND IRON BELT.

AUSTIN AND NORTHWESTERN RAILROAD.

AUSTIN TO LLANO.

Connecting at Austin with Houston and Texas Central and International and Great Northern Railroads.

LLANO, MARBLE FALLS AND BURNET

Are the best Health Resorts in Texas.

DELIGHTFUL CLIMATE.
PURE MOUNTAIN AIR.
GOOD DRINKING WATER.

Sportsmen will find plenty of good hunting and fishing.
Spend your vacation camping on the beautiful Llano river.

SEASON OF "'99,"

Three hundred camping parties, about 1,500 people in all, enjoyed the delightful mountain air and the fine hunting and fishing.

OBJECTS OF INTEREST

To be seen on the Austin and Northwestern Railroad:

"Pack Saddle Mountain," "Wilbur's Glen," "Marble Falls," "Granite Mountain," the great "Bat Caves."

The A. & N. W. R. R. extends you a hearty invitation to enjoy an "outing" on their line.

Special rates to camping parties.

Call on or write,

L. S. PALFREY.
Gen. Freight and Pass. Agt., Austin, Texas.

Beverages

The Capitol in 1890 by an unknown photographer. Landscaping near the building has been completed but not along the walkway. As finished, the Capitol was 585 feet, ten inches in length and 299 feet, ten inches wide and was 309 feet, eight inches from the basement floor to the top of the Goddess of Liberty statue. This was quite an edifice for a town with only 15,000 people.

BEVERAGES.

COFFEE—BOILED.

Scald pot well; put coffee in, allowing 1 cup of coffee to 4 or 5 cups of water, according to the strength of the coffee. Beat in a whole egg, shell and all, if eggs are plentiful, if not, use the shell only. Then wet with cold water; pour in boiling water; let boil well, and remove a few moments before serving to allow it to settle.

DRIPPED COFFEE.

Put coffee in any good dripper (don't fill entirely, as the coffee swells) ; pour on a little boiling water, at first till the grounds swell, then add boiling water gradually till the proper strength is reached. Serve at once.

COFFEE—GOOD.

Carefully roast good coffee; grind it, and for every cup of coffee wanted put into the coffee pot one tablespoon of coffee, then for every spoonful of coffee pour in one teacup of boiling water. Put the coffee pot on the stove; just let it come to a boil, and take it off.

MRS. R. C. WALKER.

COFFEE—IN LARGE QUANTITIES.

Settle coffee with white of an egg before grinding. Make little bags that will hold about ½ pound each; put in ground coffee; sew up securely, and drop in fresh boiling water. Use a large granite pan or preserving kettle, then the coffee can be dipped out into pots, and served perfectly clear.

TEA.

For general use mixed tea is best. Allow about 1 level teaspoonful to a cup of water. Scald out your pot, put in leaves, pour on boiling water (fresh and clear), put on the back of the stove, let draw a few minutes before serving.

TEA-KETTLE TEA.

One-half cup of sweet milk, ½ cup of boiling water, sugar to taste. Old fashioned drink for very old and very young folks.

SASSAFRAS TEA.

Sassafras root can be bought at all drug stores, and makes a very palatable drink.

It should be drawn with hot water like ordinary tea, and served with milk and sugar. Aside from being a delicious beverage, it is splendid for all disorders of the blood.

CHOCOLATE.

Grate 2 ounces (or 2 squares) of Baker's chocolate, add the same amount of sugar (or sweeten to taste), 1 teaspoonful of flour (leave this out if you prefer, but I like it thick) ; mix all together with a little milk, and stir into a quart of boiling milk; let boil up several times, and serve with or without whipped cream.

If rich chocolate is desired, avoid the use of water and use fresh sweet milk.

Mrs. E. G. Myers.

TOAST.

DRY TOAST.

Comparatively fresh bread is needed for dry toast. Cut in slices about one-half inch thick and toast in toaster over red hot coals, or brown quickly on the top shelf of a very hot oven; brown on both sides, crush the edges, butter, slip back for a moment in the oven, and serve immediately.

MILK TOAST.

Stale bread or cold biscuit toasted brown; put in covered dish, and pour over scalded milk, melted butter and salt. Serve when soft.

CREAM TOAST.

Same as above, only the milk is thickened with a little cornstarch or flour. Cream makes it richer, provided you have it.

FRIED BREAD.

Cut stale bread one-fourth inch thick. Allow one egg, beaten, to a pint of milk; a pinch of salt; a teaspoonful of sugar; a teaspoonful of flour, made smooth in a little of the milk, put together. Soak six slices of a loaf, turning them over in milk; put a little sweet lard on griddle, and when hot fry each slice a delicate brown on both sides. Use the pancake turner.

Some like a little cinnamon sprinkled on when taken up; pile up, keep hot and serve—*good.*

Victoria. Mrs. R. L. Dabney.

EGG TOAST.

One egg to one cup of sweet milk, a little salt. Beat the egg, add milk, dip in slices of bread till soft, and fry a nice brown.

CHEESE TOAST.

Toast fresh bread in very hot oven; remove and put grated cheese on each slice; put back in oven long enough to melt cheese, and serve with coffee at breakfast.

SOUTHERN TOAST.

Fry nice fresh bacon; drain from it most of the grease, then add enough milk for toast, let it boil up, then pour over the bacon which has been placed piece by piece on nice toasted bread.

MRS. IDA HAGERTY.

A NICE WAY TO MAKE TOAST ON A GASOLINE OR KEROSENE STOVE.

Butter slices of bread slightly on both sides. Put on very hot griddle, turn as soon as brown. This toast is softer and more crisp than browning in the oven.

TOASTED CRACKERS AND CHEESE.

Place crackers in pan, put a slice of cheese about half the size of the cracker in the center, and toast a delicate brown.

Eggs and Omelets

Interior views of the third floor Capitol corridor (top) and the entrance to the Governor's Public Room (bottom) about the time of the Capitol's opening. Most of the door and window frames are of oak and pine and the wainscoting of various native Texas woods.

EGGS AND OMELETS.

BOILED EGGS.

Put eggs in a stew pan, pour on boiling water to cover and let boil rapidly 2½ or 3 minutes for soft boiled, and serve at once.

Hard boiled eggs require twice the time.

BOILED EGGS USED TO GARNISH.

Boil eggs very hard, remove shells and skins; cut whites lengthwise in 4 or 5 strips, leaving yellow in the center. If arranged correctly they will resemble water lilies.

SHIRRED EGGS.

Use individual granite dishes that are made for this purpose, or a granite pie pan or heavy stone china plate. Butter the plate and break in carefully as many eggs as are required, place in oven, let cook three minutes, salt and pepper and serve at once.

This is the easiest way to cook eggs, and an improvement on poached or fried eggs.

FRIED EGGS.

Have hot lard in a frying pan. Break one egg at a time into a saucer; slip into the hot lard, being careful to keep them from touching.

Baste with hot lard or turn over if you prefer. Salt and pepper to taste. Serve at once.

Nice for breakfast served with broiled ham or bacon.

SCRAMBLED EGGS.

Beat eggs well, salt and pepper, pour into a hot well-greased frying pan and stir constantly.

Avoid cooking too hard.

SCRAMBLED EGGS WITH CHEESE, RICE, ONIONS OR IRISH POTATOES.

Grated or sliced cheese, one onion chopped fine, a cup of cold rice or cold boiled potatoes cut in dice, improve scrambled eggs.

When either of the above are used, put in the hot greased pan and heat well, then pour in the eggs and scramble.

BAKED EGGS.

Hard boiled eggs cut in two, either crossways or lengthways.

Remove yolks carefully, and mash smooth with butter, add salt and pepper. Place in baking dish and brown slightly on top shelf in oven.

FRENCH EGGS.

Boil hard, remove shells, roll in cracker meal and fry in butter until brown. Serve with gravy made of butter, cracker meal and a little sweet milk, salt added to the yolks.

OMELET (PLAIN).

To 6 eggs, beaten separately, add 1 teaspoon flour to the egg, as much sweet milk as the yolks (about ½ cup), salt and pepper. Beat in whites and bake in slightly greased pan, first on top of stove and then slip inside till thoroughly dry and then fold.

OMELET NO. 2.

Eight eggs, beaten separately, add 1 tablespoon of flour, salt and pepper to taste, and a half cup of sweet milk to the yolks; lastly stir in the whites well-beaten, cook on a griddle or in a buttered flat pan for a few minutes. Fold and serve at once.

FANCY OMELET.

Make same as above recipe, only after the omelet is in the pan ready to cook, sprinkle on any of the following: Parsley chopped, grated cheese, cold minced ham, one onion chopped fine, that has previously been fried in a little butter.

BREAD CRUMB OMELET.

Soak 1 cupful bread crumbs in 1 cupful of sweet milk for several hours. Add 4 eggs, beaten separately, yolks first, salt to taste, then whites and cook at once in butter.

MRS. H. B. HOUSTON.

BAKED OMELET.

Four eggs beaten together until very light.

One pint sweet milk.

One tablespoon butter.

Salt and pepper to taste.

Pour into a baking dish and cook about twenty minutes. Serve very hot.

DRESSED EGGS.

One tablespoon of flour.

One-half teaspoon of salt.

One tablespoon of butter.

One-half pint of milk, pepper and salt.

Boil eggs 15 minutes, remove the shells, cut in half crosswise, slice a little of the bottom to make them stand up. Put butter in pan, melt and add flour; add milk and stir till it boils, add salt and pepper. Stand the eggs on a heated platter, pour sauce over and serve hot. This is a nice accompaniment for roast turkey.

Bread

Alamo Monument, Austin, Texas.

The Heroes of the Alamo Monument was the first monument erected on the Capitol grounds. The monument was built by J.S. Clark of Louisville, Kentucky and was dedicated in 1891. The bronze figure of a Texan with a muzzle loading rifle is mounted atop the granite structure supported on four columns. There is also a bronze depiction of the battle of the Alamo mounted on the west face of the structure. The names of the 186 defenders of the Alamo are engraved on the inside of the four supporting columns.

BREAD.

REMARKS.

More common sense is required in bread making than in any other branch of cooking. On account of different grades of soda, cream of tartar, baking powder and yeast, it is impossible to be accurate as to the exact amount to use.

Where sour milk is used, a young cook had just as well make up her mind to taste uncooked bread, so as to ascertain whether there is not enough or too much soda, as this is the only way to succeed every time.

Always use the best of everything, to insure the best results.

YEAST CAKES.

One pint of peach leaves in a quart of water, boil down to a pint, let cool, thicken with meal and a small quantity of flour. Add one yeast cake dissolved in ½ teacup of water. Set away until it rises. Then add meal and enough flour to roll out, and cut in cakes.

Dry in the shade, turn over twice a day until perfectly dry.

MRS. L. J. STOREY.

TO MAKE GOOD YEAST.

Take 5 or 6 good sized potatoes, then pour 2 quarts of boiling water to them, also drop in a small handful of hops tied in a bag. Take potatoes out when done and mash them, take out hops, then make a teacup and a half of flour in a smooth paste and stir in the hop tea; let boil 5 minutes. Then put in the mashed potatoes, take off the fire, and put in ½ cup of good yeast or leaven. Keep in a warm place till it rises well, then tie up close and put away till needed, or make leaven.

Victoria. MRS. R. L. DABNEY.

SALT RISING BREAD.

At dinner time scald ½ teacup of meal with 1 pint of boiling milk or water. Set aside, and in the morning put into pitcher or jar ½ teaspoonful of salt, 1 pint of boiling water, a small pinch of soda. When it is milk warm add flour enough and the scalded meal to make a stiff sponge. Put the jar in warm water and keep it warm till it rises. This will take 1½ quarts of flour, and a small tablespoonful of lard. Make at once into loaves, any pan or shape you choose, and let rise; then bake in a moderate oven.

Victoria. MRS. R. L. DABNEY.

GOOD LIGHT BREAD.

One cake Fleischman's compressed yeast in 1 pint of luke warm water, when dissolved add 2 pints of warm milk, thicken with flour to a stiff batter. When it rises, in about 30 minutes, sift flour into tray, put in a kitchenspoonful of sugar, same of butter and 1 teaspoonful of salt, mix well in flour, pour in yeast, knead a long time, the longer the better, but keep as soft as possible. Mold in loaves, put in greased pan, butter the top, let rise again, and bake in moderate oven one hour.

MRS. R. J. BRACKENRIDGE.

LIGHT BREAD.

Take 1 quart of flour, 1 yeast cake dissolved in ½ cup of water, 1 tablespoonful of white sugar, ½ tablespoonful of lard worked in flour, 1 teaspoonful of salt. Make in a batch; work well. If it gets light before time to form in loaves or rolls, work a little without taking from the bucket, just push down without adding flour. An hour before baking make in loaves or rolls, let rise and bake.

In summer make up with cold water, in winter warm water.

Victoria. MRS. R. L. DABNEY.

BROWN BREAD.

Two cups of sour milk.
Two cups of sweet milk.
One scant cup of molasses.
Three cups of corn meal.
Two cups of rye or wheat flour.
Two teaspoonfuls of soda.
One teaspoonful of salt.

Put in a 2-quart basin, place in a steamer and steam 3 hours, then bake ½ hour till a light-brown crust is formed.

Victoria. MRS. R. L. DABNEY.

BROWN BREAD.

Two cups of sour milk.

One-half cup of molasses.

Three and one-half cups of Graham flour (or entire wheat).

One teaspoonful of soda.

One teaspoonful of salt.

Bake slowly one hour.

MRS. S. L. ELDRIDGE.

DELICIOUS RUSKS.

One cup of butter.

Two cups of sugar.

One pint of warm milk.

One-half yeast cake dissolved in a cup of warm water.

Stir in flour enough to make a soft dough, set to rise, add more flour, beat thoroughly and set to rise again. When light mold into biscuit, put in a warm place until light and bake in a quick oven.

MRS. GEO. W. MASSIE.

RUSK ROLLS.

Take $\frac{1}{2}$ good yeast cake and dissolve in 1 quart of luke warm water.

Cream $\frac{1}{2}$ cup of sugar and 1 cup of butter, beat 2 eggs well and add to butter and sugar $\frac{1}{4}$ teaspoonful of salt. Pour all in yeast water. Then sift in flour till you have a stiff batter, beat well, set to rise in warm place.

When light and spongy, add more flour and work for 20 minutes. Let rise again in tray; in 1 hour make in rolls. Put to rise in a greased pan for a few minutes, then bake in a moderate oven.

Doughnuts are made in the same way, only cut dough in strips, fry in boiling lard, and powder with sugar.

MRS. EDITH WEEDEN.

PALMER HOUSE ROLLS.

One quart of flour.

One egg well beaten.

One tablespoonful of butter.

One tablespoonful of sugar.

One teaspoonful of salt.

Make into a soft dough with sweet milk.   Roll about ½ inch thick, cut out, butter the top, turn one half over the other, press down with the fingers and bake as biscuit.

MISS ELLA BEDELL.

PARKER HOUSE ROLLS.

One pint of cold boiled milk.
One teaspoonful of salt.
Two quarts sifted flour.
One large tablespoonful of lard.
One-half yeast cake in a cup of warm water.
One teaspoonful of sugar.

Put flour in bowl with salt and sugar, mix, rub in lard, pour in yeast water and milk.   Then stir and knead well, pound for 15 minutes, put back in bowl, cover and set away until light.   Then roll out on board, ¼ inch thick, cut round, fold ⅓ over, let stand an hour, and bake.

Victoria.   MRS. R. L. DABNEY.

SOUR MILK BISCUIT.

Put ¼ teaspoonful of soda and ½ teaspoonful of salt into 1 pint of the best flour, and sift three times.

Rub 1 tablespoonful of best "kettle rendered" lard into the flour until perfectly smooth.   Then mix gently with 3 tablespoonfuls of good firm clabber into which has been put 3 or 4 drops of lemon juice. Mix all with a spoon and handle as little as possible.   Roll out ¼ inch thick, fold and roll again ¼ inch thick, cut and bake at once in a very quick oven.

E. C.

BAKING POWDER BISCUIT.

One quart of flour.
One tablespoonful of lard.
A pinch of salt.
Two heaping teaspoonfuls of baking powder.
Cold water enough to make a soft dough.
Bake in a quick oven.
Biscuit made in this way are very good.

MRS. R. C. WALKER.

SODA BISCUIT.

First test your sour milk and use soda accordingly, if very sour a full teaspoonful of soda to a quart of flour will not be too much.

To a quart of flour add a heaping teaspoonful of salt, a level tea-spoonful of soda and 1 tablespoonful of lard.

Sift all together. Make a hole in the middle of the flour, put in lard and pour in milk enough to work up the flour; knead smoothly. Roll ½ inch thick, cut and bake in a rather hot oven.

Tehuacana. MRS. J. J. VANNOY.

BISCUIT NO. 2.

One quart of flour.

One level teaspoonful of soda.

One teaspoonful of baking powder.

One and one-half tablespoonfuls of lard.

Flake lard in with flour, soda, baking powder and salt.

Pour in buttermilk, mix lightly, roll thin, cut, and bake in a quick oven.

MRS. D. H DOOM.

BEATEN BISCUIT.

To 1 quart of flour add 1 teaspoonful of salt, 2 tablespoonfuls of butter or lard, and mix with sweet milk.

Beat until the dough blisters, then roll and cut.

Bake a light brown. Very nice and delicate.

MRS. G. CROW.

MUFFINS.

(A simple but good recipe.)

One egg.

One tablespoonful of melted butter.

Three cups of flour.

One tablespoonful of sugar.

Three tablespoonfuls of baking powder.

Beat the egg light, add sugar and melted butter, then the flour, with sweet milk enough to make a stiff batter.

The batter must be stiff enough to drop from the spoon.

MRS. L. B. COPES.

MUFFINS NO. 2.

Two eggs beaten together, 1½ teacups of sour milk; add ½ teaspoonful of salt, ½ teaspoonful of soda, 1 level teaspoonful of baking powder, butter or lard the size of an egg. Beat in flour to make a stiff batter, and bake in well greased muffin pans in a hot oven. Have pan hot before putting in batter.

CREAM MUFFINS.

One pint of cream.

Two eggs.

Three cups of sifted flour.

One tablespoonful of melted butter.

One teaspoonful of salt.

Two teaspoonfuls of baking powder.

Beat yolks well, add cream, add this gradually to the flour. Let stand 15 minutes, add salt, melted butter, the whites well beaten, and baking powder. Mix well. Bake in muffin rings in a hot oven about 25 minutes.

Victoria. MRS. R. L. DABNEY.

SALLY LUNN.

Two cups of flour.

One-half cup of sugar.

One cup of sweet milk.

A lump of butter the size of an egg.

A pinch of salt.

Two heaping teaspoonfuls of baking powder.

Three eggs, beaten separately.

Beat yolks, add sugar and butter, then milk and flour, and lastly whites.

MRS. PAULINE DRANE.

SALLY LUNN.

Melt 2 tablespoonfuls of butter in 1 cup of warm milk, and add ⅛ of an yeast cake dissolved in two tablespoonfuls of cold water. Sift 2 cups of flour, ½ teaspoonful of salt, and 1 tablespoonful of sugar. Pour liquid mixture on this and beat well. Add 1 egg, beaten separately. Beat all thoroughly, and pour into a nice buttered cake pan.

Cover closely and let rise in a cool place over night. Bake ½ hour in a moderate oven. Turn out on a napkin, and cut at the table.

MRS. BENEDETTE B. TOBIN.

CORN MEAL BATTERCAKES.

Two cups sifted meal.

One teaspoonful of salt.

Scald just enough to dampen.

One-half teaspoonful of soda.

One teaspoonful of baking powder.

Pour on buttermilk to make rather thin batter, beat in one egg. Sift in a little flour. Bake on a hot griddle. Don't let cakes touch.

CORN MEAL MUFFINS AND WAFFLES.

Make like batter cakes, only have thicker batter and one or two more eggs.

Sweet milk and baking powder can be used if preferred.

RICE AND GRITS BATTERCAKES.

One cup of cold rice or grits; pour on a little warm water to soften, beat in 1 egg, 1 teaspoonful of salt, 1 level teaspoonful of soda, 1 teaspoonful of baking powder, 2 cups of sour milk; flour enough to make rather stiff batter.

WAFFLES.

Four eggs.

One tablespoonful of butter.

One pint of sweet milk.

One-half teaspoonful of salt.

Two teaspoonfuls of baking powder.

Flour for thick batter.

Heat irons well, grease well, and fill half full.

Use soda and sour milk if you prefer.

MRS. R. L. DABNEY.

RICE BATTER BREAD.

One scant pint of corn meal.

One pint boiling water.

One level teaspoonful of salt.

One small tablespoonful of lard.

One pint of buttermilk or sour milk.
Level teaspoonful soda (scant).
One pint of cold rice.
Four eggs, well beaten.
Bake forty-five minutes.

MRS. H. B. HOUSTON.

WAFFLES.

Beat 2 or 3 eggs, pour in 1 pint of buttermilk, add 1 level teaspoonful each of salt, soda and baking powder. (If milk is very
sour, add soda to taste.) Sift in enough flour to make rather stiff,
add 1 teaspoonful of lard to make crisp. Then beat well till batter
is very light. Bake in very hot, well greased irons, and avoid putting in too much batter.

MRS. J. K. HOLLAND.

FLANNEL CAKES.

Beat well 2 eggs; add ½ teaspoonful of salt, ½ pint of buttermilk,
½ teaspoonful of soda, 1 level teaspoonful of baking powder, flour to
make light batter. Bake on hot hoe, slightly greased.

GOOD EGG BREAD.

Sift 2 cups of meal and add a little salt, scald meal enough to
dampen (not too much), and beat in 1 egg; then pour in enough
sour milk to make a thin batter, and add ½ teaspoonful of soda.
Grease a shallow pan, have it piping hot and pour in the batter.
Bake in a hot oven.

MRS. S. P. WEISIGER.

CORN BREAD.

To 1 quart of corn meal add 1 teaspoonful of salt and 2 teaspoonfuls of baking powder. Sift all together. Now add a heaping tablespoonful of lard and then scald with boiling water, using enough
water to wet the meal; then add a pint of sour milk that has a pinch
of soda in it, enough to neutralize the acid (it is impossible to say
how much soda must be used, because it depends upon how sour the
milk is). Lastly add 4 eggs. Put in a well greased pan, and bake
in a hot oven.

MRS. ROBT. C. SHELLEY.

CORN BREAD.

To 1 quart of corn meal add ½ teacup of flour, salt to taste, 2 table-spoonfuls of baking powder, mix in the dry meal. Take a heaping tablespoonful of cottoline (lard if you prefer) and work thoroughly into the meal, with the fingers, lightly. Add enough cold water, no milk, to soften the dough. Now break in 1 egg and beat well, add enough water to make rather a thin batter. Pour into a smoking hot, well greased pan. Bake in a hot oven.

MRS. MOORE MURDOCK.

PLAIN CORN BREAD.

Sift 1 pint of meal, add a little salt, scald enough to dampen; add cold water to make thick batter.

Have ready a well greased pan, piping hot; dip your hands in cold water, mold bread in pones, place in pan; bake in a quick oven, top shelf first.

CRACKLING BREAD.

One or two cups of cracklings, chopped rather fine; pour on a cup of hot water to soften, mix in plain corn bread as above, only scald the meal with the water poured off the cracklings. Bake as above.

MRS. E. G. MYERS.

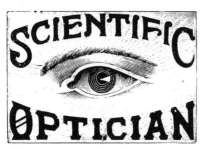

Mexican Dishes

The Capitol building in 1891 as seen by Austin photographer S.B. Hill. The newly dedicated Heroes of the Alamo Monument is shown at the right and trees have been planted along the walkway.

MEXICAN DISHES.

CHILI CON CARNE.

Cut or chop into small slices two pounds of beef, add a little chopped tallow and salt; place the above in a covered pot, in which you have previously heated 2 or 3 tablespoons of lard, and steam till about half done; now add two quarts of hot water, and one or two tablespoonfuls of Gebhardt's Eagle Chili Powder, according to strength desired; stir well, then boil slowly until meat is tender.

CHILI CON CARNE NO. 2.

Use cold beef roast or soup meat; chop fine, add a little salt, 1 level tablespoonful of flour, 1 tablespoonful of lard, and 1 tablespoonful of Gebhardt's Eagle Chili Powder. Then add a cup of warm water, and cook several minutes. Serve with frijoles.

FRIJOLES.

Soak the beans over night in weak soda water, pour off the old and add fresh water, salt, and some lard or a piece of bacon; boil until tender.

FRIJOLES, QUICK WAY TO COOK.

One pint of beans, 2 quarts of cold water, salt to taste, a small piece of bacon; boil rapidly for two hours, or until thoroughly done. Add a little more water if necessary.

BAKED FRIJOLES.

Take cold frijoles; mash perfectly smooth, put in baking dish, smooth the top with butter, and brown nicely.

TAMALES.

Boil one pound of beef and pour over some hot beef fat.

Scald thoroughly one quart of meal, adding one teaspoonful of salt and a tablespoonful of lard.

Cut off the upper end of corn shucks, and put to boil in cold water; let scalded meal and shucks cool off.

Chop the beef fine and season to taste with salt and Gebhardt's Eagle Chili Powder.

Put a thin layer of meal on shucks (leaving shucks enough to turn ends and sides under), then put a small quantity of meat in the center.

Roll the whole like a cigarette, and fold the small end of the husk.

Put a few shucks in the bottom of a pot to prevent scorching, and pack in the tamales, placing a weight on top. Cover with boiling water, add 1 tablespoon each of lard and Gebhardt's Eagle Chili Powder. Boil one hour; if water gets too low, add more.

TAMALE PIE.

Take a dressed chicken, cut up in small pieces. Put butter or sweet lard in bottom of the pot, place chicken in and brown nicely. Add 1 can of tomatoes, one large onion and two chili peppers; also a little salt and hot water; stew until tender. Thicken gravy, turn all into a deep earthen dish, drop about a dozen olives through the stew, and slice 6 hard boiled eggs over the top.

Cover all with a rich pie crust; put in oven, and bake.

Mrs. CONWAY.

OLLA PODRIDA.

Fry one small onion, cut fine, in 1 tablespoonful of butter, until it is light brown; add one pint each of green corn, okra, butter beans and tomatoes, and enough water to cook tender. Add gravy if preferred. Season highly with black and red pepper and salt. If desired, add finely chopped chicken or beef.

Mrs. CHARLES D. WALSH.

DEVILED TOMATOES.

Take two or three large firm tomatoes (not over ripe); cut in slices $\frac{1}{2}$ inch thick and lay on a sieve. Make a dressing of one tablespoon of butter and 1 tablespoon of vinegar rubbed with the yolk of one hard boiled egg, add salt to taste, a little sugar and mustard, and $\frac{1}{2}$ teaspoon of Gebhardt's Eagle Chili Powder; beat until smooth, and heat to the boiling point; take from the fire and pour upon one well beaten egg, whipping constantly. Put the tomatoes in a hot dish and pour over the dressing.

Cooked in this style, will be found an exquisite accompaniment with roasted chicken.

STUFFED SQUASH.

Boil the squash and cut them in halves, removing the seed. Take tomatoes, onions, and a small piece of garlic, and cut all very fine. Fry the mixture in a little lard. After this stuff the squash with it; then with bread crumbs, beaten fine. Fry the stuffed squash when they are ready for the table.

FACE TO FACE WITH THE MEXICANS.

CHILY HUEROS CON QUESO.

(Pepper and Eggs with Cheese.)

Toast the peppers in the fire, remove the seed, and cut into small slices. Have some hot lard in a sauce pan, into which throw a handful of chopped onions, the same of tomatoes.

Pour in water and when it is boiling break in as many eggs as you like. Put in the sliced peppers, and when on the dish ready to serve, cover the whole with grated cheese.

FACE TO FACE WITH THE MEXICANS.

CHILI SAUCE.

See Pickles, Sweet Pickles, Chow Chow and Catsup.

Soups

The Volunteer Fireman Monument dedicated on July 7, 1896 was the second monument erected on the Capitol grounds. It was paid for by The State Fireman's Association of Texas to honor those volunteer firemen who had lost their lives in the line of duty. The square granite pillar is topped by a figure of a fireman cradling a child in his left arm and holding a lantern in his right hand. On the sides of the pillar are incised the names of ninety-six volunteer fireman who lost their lives. The first name is that of Eugene T. Teats, Sr. of Austin, 1877 and the most recent, Clifford R. Harris, Rusk, 1994.

SOUPS.

~~~~~~~~

STOCK.

Take a good sized shank of beef, have the butcher crack the bone; cover with a gallon of cold water, and boil till the meat falls to pieces, or until the water has boiled down to half the quantity. Skim well. Remove meat, salt to taste, and strain.

This is the foundation for all beef and vegetable soups.

BOUILLON.

Four pounds raw beef, chopped fine, covered with 1 gallon of water; place on stove, and cook very slowly for 6 or 7 hours. For the first hour it should barely simmer, then bring gradually to a boiling point. Stir occasionally. Salt to taste. Set aside to cool, skim off the fat and squeeze out the meat. The liquor should have boiled down to two quarts; if you haven't that much, make up the amount with boiling water. Pour into a clean granite kettle; throw in a crushed egg shell and a little of the white to settle. Boil rapidly for ten minutes, then strain through an old cloth. It is a beautiful amber color and should be served very hot in glass bouillon cups, without spoons.

It is particularly nice for luncheons or dinners.

VEGETABLE SOUP.

Boil a five-cent soup bone in 2 quarts of water till meat has boiled to pieces; take out bone and add 1 small can of okra and tomatoes (mixed), 1 onion, and 1 Irish potato cut in small pieces, 3 sticks of macaroni broken in half-inch pieces, 1 tablespoon of rice; salt and pepper to taste.

When vegetables are well done, thicken with two tablespoons of flour mixed smooth with a little water.

MRS. E. G. MYERS.

3—C. B.

VEGETABLE SOUP (WHITE).

Boil soup bone 2 or 3 hours, add ½ cup finely shredded cabbage, 1 white onion chopped fine, 1 potato, and 1 turnip cut in small cubes.

When vegetables are well done, season with salt and thicken with a tablespoon of flour mixed smooth with water or milk. A half cup of sweet milk may be added to make it whiter, but it is not necessary.

GOOD BEEF SOUP.

Put a five-cent soup bone into about a gallon of cold water; boil until 3 quarts of water are left, into which put 1 teaspoon of sugar, 2 small teaspoons of salt, half a teaspoon of black pepper. Cut fine 2 small carrots, 1 large Irish potato, 1 onion (cut and fried in butter), a small pinch of nutmeg and cloves, 2 tablespoons of tomato catsup, 1 tablespoon rice, 2 pods of okra, ½ cup butter beans, ½ cup of green corn, 2 mustard leaves and 3 large sprigs of parsley cut fine; boil all till done, and serve without straining.

MRS. IDA HAGERTY.

JULIENNE SOUP.

Make stock as for any other soup.

Take 3 quarts of stock to 1 cup of each of the following vegetables: Shredded carrots, turnips, celery, the dark green outside leaves of a cabbage; a little parsley, and a long red pepper cut in small pieces. Boil until vegetables are done, salt to taste, and serve with crackers.

The different colored vegetables makes this a very pretty soup.

MRS. E. G. MYERS.

TOMATO SOUP.

Mash through a colander one large can of tomatoes, add a pinch of soda and let boil up once. Have a quart of sweet milk boiling, to which add one large spoon of butter and the tomatoes; let boil up once, then pour into a tureen and add salt and pepper to taste. Put in each soup plate five or six half-inch squares of toasted bread over which pour the soup, and serve.

MRS. IDA HAGERTY.

TOMATO SOUP.

Boil together for 15 minutes 1 quart of tomatoes, a pint of water, ½ onion, a bay leaf, ½ teaspoonful of celery seed; 1½ tablespoonfuls of butter and 3 tablespoonfuls of flour, rubbed together and added to the soup. Stir until boiling; add a teaspoonful of salt; season with black and cayenne pepper to taste.

Strain, reheat and serve with thin strips of toasted bread, biscuit or. crackers. This is delicious.

MRS. BENEDETTE B. TOBIN.

TOMATO SOUP.

Boil soup meat in one gallon of water till it falls from the bone, and add 1 can of tomatoes, 1 small onion, sliced; let boil slowly in a covered kettle 2 hours; strain and add salt and pepper to taste; mix 1 tablespoon of butter with 1 tablespoon of flour to thicken and add to the soup.

ENGLISH PEA SOUP.

One pint of shelled peas and 1 quart of water; boil well and when done skim out the peas, rub through a colander, then put back in liquor. Put in 2 cups of sweet milk and 1 tablespoon of butter, salt and pepper to taste. Thicken with a tablespoon of flour and a little water mixed smooth; let boil up, and serve.

POTATO SOUP.

One quart milk; 1 stalk of celery; 1 small onion; 4 potatoes, boiled and mashed; 1 tablespoon of butter and one of flour, creamed together; salt to taste.

Put through a sieve, and serve in a hot tureen.

FROM TEXAS COOK BOOK.

CORN SOUP.

Cut corn from cob and scrape well, add 2 quarts of water and boil 15 or 20 minutes; pour in 1 quart of sweet milk and a tablespoon of butter; salt and pepper to taste, and thicken with a little flour and milk.

BISQUE SOUP,

One can of tomatoes.

One quart of sweet milk.

Three crackers.

One tablespoon of butter.

Put milk in porcelain vessel, heat to almost boiling; add butter. Strain through a colander the tomatoes; roll crackers to a powder and add to the milk with a pinch of soda; just let boil and remove from stove.   Add salt and pepper to taste.

Mrs. L. B. Copes.

TO UTILIZE THE BONES AND SCRAPS LEFT FROM TURKEY.

Place the bones in a good sized stewpan and cover with cold water; let them boil until the water has become a rich stock.   Then add a quart of milk, a few pieces of celery, a tablespoon of butter, salt and pepper to taste.   This makes an excellent white soup.

CHICKEN SOUP.

Cut up chicken in small pieces; put on to boil in a gallon of salt water; when tender, remove the chicken and put ½ cup of rice in the broth, and boil till rice is done; add 1 tablespoon of butter, black pepper, and 2 cups of sweet milk; thicken with a tablespoon of flour mixed smooth with a little milk.

The chicken may be served with cream gravy or made into a pie.

CHICKEN GUMBO.

Six good sized tomatoes, scald, peel, and slice up; 1 quart okra, slice in small rings; 2 onions, sliced; season and fry all well done. Chicken or veal cut in small pieces, flour and fry in hot fat; put in 2 quarts of boiling water and let simmer 2 or 3 hours.   Serve with slices of lemon.

Mrs. A. Walthersdorf.

CHICKEN GUMBO NO. 2.

Fry one chicken, then, in the hot lard where chicken has been fried, fry one quart of okra, cut in thin slices, salted and floured. Cut chicken off the bones, and mince (not too fine) ; then put back in frying pan with the okra; add 1 quart boiling water, let cook five minutes; then add 1 pint sweet milk, 1 tablespoon of butter, salt and pepper.   If it is not thick enough add a little flour and water smoothed together.

Mrs. E. G. Myers.

MOCK TURTLE SOUP.

Boil the soup meat until very tender, then strain off the liquor; chop a small onion in very small pieces and fry a light brown.   Have a teacup of browned flour, mix gradually into the liquor, put in the onion, a dozen allspice, $\frac{1}{2}$ dozen cloves, 4 little red peppers, and season with salt and pepper. Let all boil together for half an hour; have 2 or 3 hard boiled eggs, chopped fine, in the tureen. Then when the soup is poured in the tureen add two tablespoons of wine or the juice of lemon.

Mrs. T. W. House, in *Texas Cook Book.*

The Confederate Monument was dedicated in 1903 to the memory of the Confederate dead of all the Confederate States. The massive granite base has four seven-foot tall figures at each corner that represent the Infantry, Cavalry, Artillery and Navy military arms of the Confederacy. A seven foot, nine inch central figure at the top represents Jefferson Davis, President of the Confederacy. The sculptor of the figures was Pompeo Coppini and the monument's builder was Frank Teich of San Antonio.

FISH.

~~~~~~~~

FISH CHOWDER.

Take a fresh red fish of 3 or 4 pounds, clean it well, cut in pieces three inches square. Place in the bottom of your dinner pot 5 or 6 slices of salt pork, fry brown; then add three onions, sliced thin, and fry those brown.

Remove the kettle from the fire, and place on the onions and pork a layer of fish, sprinkle over a little salt and pepper, then a layer of pared and sliced potatoes, continuing to alternate layers of fish and potatoes till the fish is used up. Cover with water and let boil for half hour. Pound six biscuits or crackers as fine as meal and pour into the pot, and lastly add a pint of milk or sweet cream; let it scald well, and serve.

This is nice. TEXAS COOK BOOK.

BAKED FISH WITH SAUCE.

Take a fish weighing 5 or 6 pounds—red snapper is good. Wash thoroughly, wipe dry.

Sprinkle inside and out with salt and pepper; put into a large baking pan long enough to lay flat, sprinkle generously with flour, and lay small pieces of butter on top the fish. Pour boiling water around the fish until it is half covered. Bake one hour, or more if the fish is larger than 6 pounds. Baste with the gravy constantly while baking; it should be well browned.

Sauce.—Boil 2 eggs until hard, remove shell, and place in cold water.

Put into a porcelain sauce pan 1 pint of milk, rub together two tablespoonfuls of butter and one of flour. When the milk is hot, not boiling, add flour and butter and let it thicken. Season with salt and pepper. Chop the eggs fine and add when just ready to serve.

The sauce can be varied by adding capers or chopped pickles. Serve as soon as possible after making.

MRS. L. B. COPES.

ANOTHER SAUCE FOR BAKED FISH.

If there is not enough gravy from the water and butter from which the basting has been done, add a little more hot water and butter and the juice of a lemon, with a tablespoonful of browned flour rubbed smooth in cold water; bring to a boil, and serve hot. A little chopped parsley or mint will add relish.

MISS ARMOR D. HEAD.

WHITE SAUCE.

One pint of milk, let come to a boil. Cream together 2 tablespoonfuls of butter and 2 of flour; pour milk on slowly, stirring perfectly smooth; season with salt and pepper, a little onion juice, and a few sprigs of parsley chopped fine. Put back on the stove; stir constantly till it thickens.

SUGGESTIONS FOR BAKED FISH.

Place fish on a tin sheet, well greased, in the bottom of the baking pan, as it can be more easily slipped onto the dish when ready to serve. Baked fish is sometimes stuffed with a dressing the same as for turkey. Thin slices of bacon placed on the fish improves the flavor.

BOILED WHITE FISH WITH TARTAR SAUCE.

Prepare the fish as for broiling, laying it open; put into a dripping pan with the back down, nearly cover with water.

For one fish use 2 tablespoonfuls of salt, cover tight, and simmer (don't boil) for half hour.

Dress with tartar sauce, and garnish with hard boiled eggs.

TARTAR SAUCE.

The raw yolks of two eggs.
One-half teacup of pure olive oil.
Three tablespoonfuls of vinegar.
One tablespoonful of made mustard.
One teaspoonful of sugar.
One-fourth teaspoonful of pepper.
One tablespoonful of salt.
One tablespoonful of onion juice.
One tablespoonful of chopped cucumber pickle.

Put together the same as for mayonnaise, adding the chopped ingredients last.

MRS. W. H. TOBIN.

FRIED FISH.

Cut up the fish avoiding the bones as much as possible. Salt and pepper well, roll in corn meal, fry in boiling lard flesh side down.

If very small fish are used they should be fried very brown and crisp.

Another equally nice way is to dip pieces of fish in beaten egg, then in cracker meal, before frying.

A NICE WAY TO FRY FISH.

Put a tablespoonful of Durkee's Salad Dressing in a saucer, dip in a basting brush and brush evenly over the fish, dredge with corn meal, and fry a golden brown.

MRS. M. E. COLLARD.

BROILED FISH.

Grease both sides of a double wire broiler with sweet fresh lard or butter, lay in the fish, flesh side down, and broil over very red coals. If fish is thick, brown nicely in broiler, then slip on to well greased tin sheet, place in pan, and cook in oven till done. Season with drawn butter, pepper and salt, or one of the sauces for fish.

Garnish the dish with curly parsley and slices of lemon.

MRS. E. G. MYERS.

BARBECUED FISH.

Salt the fish, put in baking pan, cover with boiling water, boil slowly till almost done, then pour off nearly all of the water and add sauce made of a cup of vinegar, a tablespoonful of butter, $\frac{1}{2}$ teaspoonful black pepper, and a little Worcester sauce; baste till well done and nicely brown.

CREAMED FISH.

Boil red fish until done, tear into flakes with the fingers, cover with a white sauce, sprinkle with bread crumbs, and bake in scallop shell.

MRS. RECTOR THOMPSON.

BAKED SALMON.

To one can of salmon add 3 grated crackers, butter the size of an egg, pepper and salt to taste. Make into a large roll, and bake a delicate brown.

Serve with slices of lemon on a lettuce leaf, or garnish with parsley.

MRS. L. B. COPES.

CRABS STUFFED WITH MUSHROOMS.

Make a highly seasoned white sauce, flavored with lemon. Mix the contents of two cans of crab meat and equal quantity of mushrooms. Add to this the mashed yolks of 4 hard boiled eggs, and enough sauce to make a stiff mixture.

Fill the shells, baste the top with the whites of eggs, sprinkle with bread crumbs, and fry two at a time in a basket.

MRS. WALTER WILCOX.

FISH CHOPS.

One pound or one pint of fish.
One teaspoonful of salt.
One-half teaspoonful of pepper.
One-half teaspoonful of onion juice.
One tablespoonful of butter.
Three tablespoonfuls of flour.
One tablespoonful of chopped parsley.
One cupful of milk or cream.
Yolks of 2 eggs.

Put in a double boiler 1 cupful of cream or milk; when scalded stir into it the butter and flour rubbed smooth, and cook for five minutes. Remove from the fire, and mix in, stirring all the time, the beaten yolks of 2 eggs, put again on the fire and stir until it thickens.

Take 1 pound or 1 pint of shredded boiled fish, sprinkle over it 1 teaspoonful of salt, ½ teaspoonful of pepper, 1 tablespoon of chopped parsley, 10 drops of lemon juice. Mix the seasoned fish with the white sauce, then spread on a dish and set aside for several hours to cool and stiffen. It will not be difficult to mold if it stands long enough. Take a tablespoonful of the mixture in the hands, and mold into the form of chops, round at one end and pointed at the other.

Roll the chop in crumbs, then in beaten egg, then in coarse bread crumbs grated from the loaf.

After the chops are molded let them stand for a while to stiffen before frying. Place them in a basket, four at a time, and immerse in hot fat until an amber color. Place on a paper to dry. When all are done pierce a small hole in pointed end with a fork, and insert a sprig of parsley. Dress on a napkin, and serve with tomato or Hollandaise sauce. Any kind of fish may be used for chops.

Mrs. A. S. Walker.

HOLLANDAISE SAUCE.

Cream $\frac{1}{2}$ cup of butter, beat in the yolks of 2 eggs, one at a time, the juice of half a lemon, red pepper and salt to taste. Place the bowl in a sauce pan of boiling water, beat constantly; when it begins to thicken add $\frac{1}{2}$ cup of boiling water; take off when as thick as custard.

CREAM CELERY SAUCE.

One large bunch of celery cut fine, barely cover with water and cook slowly (simmer) 1 hour. Cream 2 tablespoons of flour and 4 of butter; add salt and pepper, and a pint of sweet cream or rich milk; let boil up, and serve at once.

SALMON CROQUETTES.

One can of salmon.

One pint of mashed Irish potatoes.

Two eggs.

One tablespoonful of butter.

Salt and pepper to taste.

Mix well together and mold in the shape of pears, fry in boiling lard until a golden brown, take out and insert a clove in the end. This is a pretty luncheon dish.

Mrs. A. S. Rutherford.

SALMON CROQUETTES.

Two pints of salmon.

One-half teacup of cream or milk.

Three tablespoonfuls of butter.

Two tablespoonfuls of flour.

Four eggs.

Salt and pepper to taste.

One pint of bread crumbs.

Melt butter and mix with flour till smooth.

Chop the salmon fine.

Put cream or milk on fire, and, when it gets to the boiling point, stir in the butter and flour, salmon and seasoning. Let all boil 2 or 3 minutes; then stir in two eggs, well beaten, and take from the fire. Set aside to cool. As soon as cool shape into croquettes, dip into the beaten eggs (use the other two), then in cracker crumbs and fry in hot lard, having enough in the pan to entirely cover the croquette.

MRS. LANSING B. FONTAINE.

SALMON CROQUETTES.

Mix together one can of salmon, 2 cups of bread crumbs, 3 eggs, and season to taste with salt and pepper. Have ready the whipped white of one egg, into which dip the salmon mixture after molding into croquettes. Then roll in bread crumbs, and fry in smoking hot fat until a delicate brown.

SALMON CROQUELLS.

Take 1 can of salmon, drain off the juice.

Put into a bowl 2 cups of cold mashed potatoes, 2 eggs, and add the salmon. Mix the whole with a potato masher; add a little salt and pepper.

Mold into oblong balls, dip in beaten egg, then in cracker meal. Fry a delicate brown, place on brown paper to absorb the fat, serve hot.

MRS. L. B. COPES.

SALMON CROQUELLS WITH MUSHROOMS.

Four cans of salmon.

Three cans of mushrooms.

Pick the salmon to pieces, chop the mushrooms, and mix together. Salt and pepper to taste.

Make a cream sauce of 1 pint of cream, seasoned with red pepper and thickened like a custard with the yolks of 3 eggs. When the sauce is on the boiling point, stir in the salmon and mushrooms and let come to a boil. Have shells ready in a pan; fill with the mixture, and over each sprinkle grated cheese. Put in oven and brown. Serve hot with water biscuit and olives.

San Angelo.   MRS. A. J. BAKER.

CODFISH CROQUETTES.

Boil shredded codfish slowly till tender. Boil potatoes till well done, and cream lightly with butter; add salt and pepper. While hot, mix in codfish. Use twice as much potatoes as codfish. Form in cakes, dredge with flour, and fry in boiling fat.

MRS. EDITH WEEDEN.

CODFISH ON TOAST.

Pick the fish in small pieces and put into cold water.

Let come to a boil, then strain in a colander, put into the skillet again with cold milk, season with butter and pepper. Stir smoothly one tablespoonful of flour with a little cold milk, add, and let boil a moment, then serve on buttered toast.

TEXAS COOK BOOK.

HOW TO COOK SHAD.

Lay on back and split rib off the backbone on each side, place on earthen dish on back, cover with vinegar and let stand 2 to 4 hours. Fry in the usual way, and when done it will be boneless.

This is vouched for by a prominent young attorney of Austin.

Oysters

STATE CAPITOL

In this 1904 view of the Capitol, a buggy is about to pass through the stone columns onto Eleventh Street. These stone columns were later moved to the State Cemetery. Also visible is the towering Volunteer Fireman Monument, the Confederate Monument and near the Capitol, the Heroes of the Alamo Monument.

OYSTERS.

RAW OYSTERS, A PRETTY WAY TO SERVE.

Put oysters and a large round or square platter, or silver waiter on ice an hour before using.

Take a clear solid block of ice, about 15 or 20 pounds, and melt a cavity in the center of the top by pouring on boiling water, being careful to pour in the center of the block, and keep pouring the water off till the cavity is large enough to hold the oysters.

Decorate the oysters with slices of lemon. Place ice in the center of the ice cold platter on some folded napkins just as you are ready to serve. Cover the outer edges of the platter with parsley or smilax and mingle in sweet peas, violets or carnations, according to the colors you are using for decorations. This makes a very pretty center piece for a table, and a beautiful effect is given by running ribbons from this center piece to each plate, with a souvenir bouquet at the end.

Mrs. E. G. Myers.

OYSTER SOUP.

Put 1 quart of oysters in a colander, pour over them a cup of cold water, drain into a kettle, add 1 quart of sweet milk; let it come to a boil; drop in the oysters just long enough for the edges to curl; add a tablespoonful of butter, salt and pepper to taste, and a few crackers broken in small pieces.

CANNED OYSTER SOUP.

These are really better for soup than the fresh, provided you get a nice quality.

Scald 1 quart of milk, pour in the oysters and liquor, season with butter, salt and pepper; let boil up a few times; thicken with cracker crumbs, and serve at once.

OYSTER STEW.

Make the same as soup, only add more crackers and less milk, and serve in saucers.

OYSTER PIE.

Line a baking dish with a rich paste. Put in a layer of oysters (canned are just as good as fresh), salt and pepper. Then a layer of hard boiled eggs, chopped fine or sliced. Season with salt, pepper and small lumps of butter. Continue to alternate till the dish is nearly full. Pour in oyster liquor, cover with pastry, cut a cross in the center, and a few minutes before taking out pour in a little sweet milk. Brown nicely, and serve hot.

MRS. SUE E. VANNOY.

ESCALLOPED OYSTERS.

Two dozen oysters is enough for an ordinary dish.

Butter a baking dish well, put in a layer of crackers (salted snow flakes are best), a few lumps of butter, then a layer of oysters, sprinkle with salt and pepper. Alternate till the dish is nearly full; let the top layer be cracker crumbs, plentifully sprinkled with bits of butter. Before putting on this layer pour in oyster liquor, and sweet milk enough to thoroughly moisten. Bake in rather quick oven for three-quarters of an hour. Serve at once, as it is liable to fall.

This is good. MRS. E. G. MYERS.

FRIED OYSTERS.

If you haven't a frying basket, get one; they are too cheap and convenient to do without.

Roll oysters in cracker crumbs or corn meal, seasoned with salt and pepper; put in basket and plunge in boiling fat till a delicate brown.

Dip in beaten egg before rolling in cracker crumbs if you prefer.

OYSTER CROQUETTES.

One pint of oysters.

One-half pint of ground veal.

One pint of cracker crumbs.

Two eggs.

Two tablespoonfuls of butter.

Salt and pepper, using a little red pepper.

Chop the oysters fine and drain off the juice. Wet the cracker crumbs in the juice; melt the butter. Mix the oysters, cracker crumbs, veal, butter and one egg together. If too soft to shape, add more crumbs; but the croquettes should be quite soft. Shape, dip in the other egg (well beaten) and crumbs, and fry.

MRS. LANSING B. FONTAINE.

OYSTER FILLING FOR PATTIES.

One tablespoonful of butter.
One tablespoonful of flour.
One teacup of cream or milk.
Yolks of 2 eggs.
Dash of cayenne.
Dash of mace.
Scald the oysters in their liquor. Drain, and cut each into four pieces. Put butter into sauce pan, when melted add flour; cook, but don't brown; then add the milk and oyster juice, and stir till smooth; then add the pieces of oysters, while hot; stir till smooth adding seasoning.

Remove from fire and add the beaten yolks of the two eggs, stirring hard. Place on the fire again, and stir till it thickens. Heat the patty crusts,* fill while hot, and serve at once.

Recommended by MRS. LANSING B. FONTAINE.

LITTLE PIGS IN BLANKETS.

Use large oysters, salt and pepper. Get the canned breakfast bacon, ready sliced. Wrap an oyster in a slice of bacon, and fasten with a small toothpick. Broil on a hot baker till the bacon is brown and crisp; serve on buttered toast or on a dish garnished with parsley.

ROASTED OYSTERS ON TOAST.

Eighteen large oysters or thirty small ones, 1 teaspoonful of flour, 1 tablespoonful of butter, salt, pepper and three slices of toast. Have the toast buttered and on a hot dish.

Put the butter in a small sauce pan, and, when hot, add the dry flour. Stir until smooth, but not brown; then add the cream, and let boil up once.

Put the oysters (in their own liquor) into a hot oven for three minutes, then add them to the cream. Season, and pour over the toast. Garnish the dish with thin slices of lemon, and serve very hot. It is nice for luncheon or tea.

MISS PARLOA'S NEW COOK BOOK.

*See Puff Paste, in Pastry.
4—C. B.

Fowls and Game

The Austin skyline as seen from South of the Colorado River in 1906. At the left of the Capitol in the distance is the Main Building at the University of Texas. To the right can be seen the Driskill Hotel and St. Mary's Academy. The moonlight towers dot the horizon.

FOWLS AND GAME.

ROAST TURKEY.

Wash turkey well with weak soda water, rub inside and out with salt and pepper. Unless very young, it is best to steam for 1 or 2 hours, or until tender. Make a dressing with equal parts of cold egg bread and light bread or biscuit; moisten with turkey liquor. Cut up an onion in a tablespoon of melted butter, and fry; then add 1 level teaspoonful of salt and black pepper, and 2 eggs well beaten. Mix all together lightly, and stuff the fowl.

Sift a little flour over the turkey, and enough in the pan to thicken the gravy. Baste with the liquor, and bake until brown.

Cut up the giblets in the gravy.

TURKEY DRESSED WITH OYSTERS.

For a 10-pound turkey take 2 pounds of bread crumbs, $\frac{1}{2}$ cup of butter (cut in bits not melted), pepper, salt, a little parsley, or summer savory, if liked; mix thoroughly.

Rub the turkey well, inside and out, with salt and pepper; then fill with first a spoonful of crumbs, then a few well drained oysters, using a pint to the turkey. Strain the oyster liquor and use to baste the turkey. Cook the giblets, and chop fine for the gravy.

A fowl of this size will require for roasting 3 hours in a moderate oven.

Mrs. Geo. S. Criser.

CELERY DRESSING.

One quart of bread crumbs.
One-half bunch of celery.
Two tablespoons of butter.
Two eggs.
Two teaspoons of salt, and 1 of pepper.
Mix lightly, and stuff the fowl.

OTHER FOWLS TO ROAST.

Use either of the turkey dressings, and bake in the same manner, only use more onions for duck, or stuff entirely with onions.

When a fowl is tough it is best to steam it tender, but put a pie pan in the bottom of the pot before putting in the fowl to prevent scorching. Steam in as little water as possible.

BOILED CHICKEN.

Boil a chicken until thoroughly tender, salt well and serve with sauce made of a tablespoonful of vinegar, $1\frac{1}{2}$ cups of water, $\frac{1}{2}$ cup of butter, salt and pepper to taste; a little flour to thicken. Cook well and pour over chicken.

CREAMED CHICKEN.

Cut up chicken, season with salt and pepper; pour over it 1 cup of sweet cream or 1 cup of milk, with a tablespoon of butter and a little flour. Cover and bake until tender; remove cover, and brown. Make more gravy if necessary.

PRESSED CHICKEN.

Take young tender fowls, boil until perfectly done, pick from the bones and chop as fine as for salad. Then season with butter, salt, pepper and celery; work together and put in a mold, with heavy weight upon it to press. When perfectly cold turn out and slice with a sharp knife.

MRS. J. G. BOOTH.

SMOTHERED CHICKEN OR BIRDS.

Split down the back, wash well, salt and pepper; put in pan with the breast up; unless very fat put thin slices of breakfast bacon between the wings and limbs. Sift on a little flour, pour on hot water enough to half cover, and baste well. Bake in a moderate oven. When nearly ready to take out, add a tablespoonful of butter and a cup of sweet milk.

FRIED CHICKEN.

Cut up in 10 or 12 pieces, salt and pepper, and dredge with flour. Fry in hot fat, not too fast; turn often to prevent burning, and allow to get well done.

If the chicken is small, dip in beaten egg, then roll in cracker crumbs before frying, and it will look larger.

BROILED CHICKEN.

Cut in halves or quarters; salt. Grease double broiler and lay on chicken. Broil gradually, don't burn, and baste with drawn butter and a little vinegar or lemon juice. Be sure it is well done; serve on platter, with the drawn butter sauce, and garnish with sliced lemon and parsley, or on buttered toast.

QUAIL ON TOAST.

Have the quails, or any other bird, dressed and opened in the back. Place in a large baking pan on their breasts, add a tablespoonful of butter to two quails, and a very little hot water. Cook in a covered pan inside the stove until nearly done, then season with salt and pepper, turn over and cook until done.

Have ready toasted light bread, dip in a pan of hot salt water, remove quickly with a batter cake turner to a hot platter. Place a bird on each piece of toast, and pour over them a dressing made from the gravy in which the birds were cooked to which has been added a teaspoonful of browned flour, a teaspoonful of butter and a half teaspoonful of Worcester sauce.

MRS. IDA HAGERTY.

CHICKEN PIE.

Make light pastry, adding a little more lard than is used in biscuit. Cut up in small pieces one frying sized chicken.

Line the sides of a deep pan with pastry, then put a layer of chicken in the bottom of pan; season each layer with salt, pepper and bits of butter. Then cover chicken with pastry, rolled thin and cut in strips or squares. Continue to alternate till all the chicken is used. Then cover the top with a sheet of pastry, print around the edges, cut a cross in the center, and fill with boiling water. Put in the oven and bake until well done; if you find it drying out, add a little more boiling water. Just before serving pour in about ½ cup of sweet milk, this makes delicious gravy.

If grown chickens are used for pie, they should be parboiled first. Tehuacana.   MRS. SUE E. VANNOY.

STEWED CHICKEN.

Cut up in small pieces, boil in salt water till tender; roll biscuit dough out thin, cut in strips, dust with flour, drop in with the boiling chicken; let cook till well done, add a little milk, butter and pepper.

CHICKEN CROQUETTES.

Boil 2 chickens until very tender, mince fine, and season with pepper, salt and ½ pint of cream or soup stock. The yolks of 2 eggs and 1½ cups of boiled rice mixed with the meat, and rolled in croquettes one inch wide and three inches long. Then roll in cracker crumbs and fry in hot lard to a nice brown. Serve in flat dish with boiled rice so that every grain is separate.

MRS. GEO. W. LITTLEFIELD.

CHICKEN CROQUETTES NO. 2.

Put 1 cup of cream or rich stock to boil in a sauce pan; mix 3 tablespoonfuls of butter with 1 of flour, and stir into the cream; then stir in 1 pint of chicken, chopped fine, and seasoned with salt and pepper. Let boil up once or twice and add 2 well beaten eggs, take off at once and let cool. Mix in bread crumbs to make stiff enough to shape in croquettes, dip in beaten egg, roll in bread crumbs, and fry in plenty of hot fat.

MRS. E. G. MYERS.

QUAILS.

Wash thoroughly a teacup of white grits, salt to taste, and cook in double boiler. When done pour in flat shallow dish, or pans to the depth of an inch; let cool, and cut in disks 5 inches in diameter. Prepare 6 quails, cut them open in back, wash thoroughly in cold water, dry on fresh towel; season with salt, a pinch of red pepper and lard well with butter. Place a half of a lemon on each disk of grits. Place the quail, breast up, on the disk and put thin slips of fat bacon over the breast. Cut stiff white paper the proper sizes for disks, lard well, and arrange in baking pan under each disk. A covered roasting pan is always necessary, but you may place a well fitting pan or cover of any description over the one containing the quails. An even temperature, not too quick, will roast the birds to perfection in 40 minutes. The last ten minutes remove the upper pan, and baste constantly with a sauce composed of a teaspoon of lemon juice, a tablespoon of butter, and 2 tablespoons of hot water. Brown, and serve.

Mrs. Moore Murdock.

CANVAS-BACK, AND OTHER GAME DUCKS.

The birds should always be dressed and placed in a sweet, cool spot the night before. Having drawn the ducks, wipe out with a clean damp cloth, avoiding the use of water as it destroys the game flavor. For dressing take a quart of large chestnuts; shell and blanch in boiling hot water until the husks part from the kernels, cut, and pound to a smooth paste. This will be sufficient for 2 ducks. Take a slice of onion and pass it about the inside of the ducks, and squeeze a half lemon over them, inside and out. Work into the chestnut paste a tablespoon of butter. Salt and pepper the ducks, and insert the dressing. Tie down the legs to give the birds an elegant appearance on the serving platter; lard well with cottoline or butter; put in a double roasting pan and roast slowly until tender, basting constantly for the last half hour, with top pan removed, or until brown. Do not fill roasting pan deeper than an inch with cold water at the beginning. It is better to add small quantities of boiling water as the original basting evaporates. Serve with brown giblet sauce.

Mrs. Moore Murdock.

Meats, Croquettes and Hash

The Terry Texas Ranger Monument was erected in 1907 by the surviving comrades of the Eighth Texas Cavalry, better known as "Terry's Texas Rangers." The granite base is topped by a fourteen foot tall bronze depicting a Ranger with his rifle at the ready. Pompeo Coppini was the sculptor and Lucas and Meier, the builders of the monument.

MEATS, CROQUETTES AND HASH.

All salt meats should be put on in cold water, and all fresh meat, except meat for soup, in boiling water, as the boiling water cooks the outside of the roast at once and closes the pores so that the juices are retained. Never stick a fork in fresh meat when cooking, as that lets out the juice. Use a spoon to turn it or stick the fork in the fat part.

PICKLED BEEF.

Cut up, sprinkle with salt, and spread it out for the night. Mix ½ gallon of salt, 2 pounds of sugar, 2 ounces saltpetre to 100 pounds of beef. Rub each piece well with the mixture, and place in a clean barrel. Make a brine of rain water and salt, strong enough to float an egg. If you cannot get rain water, then boil the kind you have. Pour the brine in the barrel until it covers the meat. Then weight it down with clean rocks or other good weights. If the brine becomes bloody, take out and boil it; skim it, and add fresh brine until meat is covered. Begin to use as soon as you please.

MRS. L. J. STOREY.

PICKLED PORK.

Twenty-four pounds of salt, 16 gallons water, 2 pounds brown sugar, 4 ounces saltpetre; boil all, and skim it until quite clear, and let it be cold before used.

Victoria. MRS. R. L. DABNEY.

HOW TO CURE MEAT.

Salt your beef; let it stand 24 hours. To 5 gallons of water put 5 quarts of salt, 2 pounds of brown sugar, 2 tablespoons of saltpetre; boil and simmer until clear, then, when cool, pour over meat.

CURING HAMS.

For each ham allow a teaspoonful of saltpetre, the same of red pepper; put in a dish and put molasses to make a thick paste; rub well each ham with the mixture, and salt them down. After 5 or 6 weeks shake off the loose salt, rub well with hickory ashes, hang and smoke with cobs or hickory once a day for 4 weeks. When needed for the table cook 4 hours.

Victoria.　　　　　　　　　　　MRS. R. L. DABNEY.

SAUSAGE.

Eighteen pounds of lean and 12 pounds of fat pork, 9 tablespoons of salt and 6 of pepper, 4 of sage. Grind in sausage grinder.

Victoria.　　　　　　　　　　　MRS. R. L. DABNEY.

BOILED HAM.

Put a handful of nice new hay into a pot of cold water; when this comes to a boil lay on the ham, over which put another wisp of hay. Let boil until ham is done. Remove from kettle, peel off the skin and pare off all discolorations; then dust the top of the ham liberally with flour or cracker crumbs, a little cinnamon, a large teaspoonful of sugar, and a quarter of a teaspoonful of pepper. Put in oven and bake till brown. The new hay gives a delicious flavor.

MRS. IDA HAGERTY.

DELICIOUS ROAST—FRENCH WAY.

Take a 4-pound beef roast, wipe dry, flour well; put a kitchen spoon of lard in a deep pot and when boiling hot put in the roast, and cover close. When it browns turn over. While browning mix 2 small onions, chopped fine; 2 slices of lemon, cut fine; 4 or 5 cloves and several slices of tomatoes, and put in pot. In case it is too dry, add a cup of water—use as little water as possible. Set on back of stove and steam for 2 or 3 hours, turning to keep from burning.

MRS. BURT MCDONALD.

ANOTHER WAY.

Wash and salt a large rib roast. Have a pot with a large spoon of hot lard; drop in the roast, and cover. When brown on one side, turn. Add 2 or 3 tomatoes, ½ lemon and 1 large onion sliced; allow them time to brown, and cover the roast with boiling water. Let boil hard till the roast is tender and the water has cooked down to a gravy. This has a most delicious flavor, and takes half the time to prepare it.

MRS. SAM WEISIGER.

ROAST BEEF.

Put on in boiling salt water, and boil hard till tender. Remove and put in baking pan; dust with flour spread on a little lard, unless very fat; pepper to taste, and a little onion if preferred. Pour over a little of the liquor and brown in oven, basting occasionally. Use the remaining liquor for making soup. If the roast is very tender it will not require parboiling, but bake as above, in a moderate oven.

ROAST PORK.

Ham or shoulder is preferable, but any nice piece will do. Put on in boiling salt water and keep boiling till meat is tender. Bake till brown in oven. Sweet potatoes, quartered, parboiled and baked around the pork is a nice addition.

FILLET OF VEAL.

Have fillet prepared at the butchers. Fill with a dressing made the same as for turkey; put in baking pan, lard and flour the top, pour over it enough water to keep from burning and bake a nice brown or till well done.

MRS. E. G. MYERS.

MOCK DUCK.

Spread dressing as for turkey on a thick round of beef steak, roll up, tie and roast.

Victoria. MRS. R. L. DABNEY.

VEAL LOAF.

Two pounds of veal and 1½ of fresh pork chopped fine, 3 eggs, 3 soda crackers, rolled fine, pepper and salt; spice and nutmeg if you like; mix well; put in a pan, press hard and bake for 5 hours. This is good.

VEAL LOAF NO. 2.

Three pounds lean veal, ½ pound salt pork, ½ grated nutmeg, 1 onion, butter the size of an egg, 2 eggs, 1 small teacup sweet milk, some red pepper. Grease pan well, press firmly in pan and graze with cracker crumbs. Bake slowly. Add sauce if you like.

Victoria. MRS. R. L. DABNEY.

BEEF ROLL.

Two pounds steak, ground; 8 crackers, rolled fine; 2 eggs; ½ cup of sweet milk; salt and pepper to taste. Mix all together and make into roll; place in your biscuit pan and on top of it place about four thin slices of breakfast bacon. Bake.

MRS. JOHN A. BROWN.

BEEF HEART.

In the morning put the heart in weak brine. In the evening change to another brine. Next morning put to cook in boiling water, and cook 3 hours; when tender, have a dressing of bread crumbs and stuff it. Put in oven and cook 25 minutes. When cold slice thin, season with more salt and pepper if you like. Keep water enough on when cooking to baste.

Victoria.   MRS. R. L. DABNEY.

SCRAPPLE.

An excellent way to cook a hog's head. Boil a hog's head till it falls to pieces. Strain the liquor that it is cooked in, and put back in the pot. Pick the meat from the bones and put back in the liquor with a cup and a half of sifted meal, a handful of powdered sage, 1 heaping teaspoonful of black pepper, ½ teaspoonful of red pepper, salt to taste. Cook till meal is done, stirring constantly to avoid scorching. Pour up in a mould, avoiding tin vessels. When congealed, slice and fry to a crisp brown, but not too greasy. This is excellent.

Tehuacana.   MRS. S. E. VANNOY.

A GOOD WAY TO FRY STEAK.

Chop the meat fine, dip in water; after taking out, salt and pepper and dredge well with flour. Fry in boiling hot lard, turning often to keep from burning before it gets done.

BROILED STEAK.

Have a thick steak for broiling. Trim off the edges, sprinkle with pepper and salt and lay in a double wire broiler, over clear coals, turning to keep from burning. Do not stick a fork into the meat as it will let out the juice. Serve on a hot dish, with plenty of butter. When there is no convenience for broiling, heat the frying pan very hot and sprinkle with salt and lay in the steak. Turn frequently.

HAM STEAKS.

Put large slices of ham in a frying pan with ½ cup of water; when the water has boiled away, and the 'ham is a light brown, sprinkle with flour; add a teacup of cream with a little butter, mustard and cayenne pepper; boil together.

Recommended by

Mrs. M. E. Collard.

HAMBURG STEAK.

(For Breakfast or Supper.)

To make this it is necessary to have a meat chopper. Grind in this one pound of steak, after removing bone and gristle; place a frying pan on the stove, with two spoons of butter; when hot, put in the chopped meat, sift over it a small quantity of flour, add pepper and salt; when the meat is cooked thoroughly, stirring all the while, add 1 cup of milk and half a cup of hot water; let boil up and pour over slices of buttered toast.

HAMBURG STEAK.

(Suitable for Dinner.)

Take a pound of round steak, grind in meat chopper; also one small onion; season with salt and pepper. Make into cakes the size of a biscuit, flat so they will cook through, place in frying pan on the stove with 2 tablespoons of butter and lard mixed; when hot put in cakes of meat, and fry slowly. These are very nice with the addition of tomato sauce, made as follows: 1 can tomatoes, 1 onion sliced fine, pinch of cloves, pepper and salt. Boil all together, take from fire and strain into another vessel. Melt an ounce of butter, and, as it melts, stir into it a tablespoon of flour, let brown, mix in the strained tomato pulp with it, and it is ready for use.

Mrs. L. B. Copes.

SCOTCH COLLOPS WITH VEAL.

Cut the remains of some cold roast veal about a thickness of cutlets; flour the meat well, and fry a light brown color in butter; dredge again with flour, and add ½ pint of water, pouring in by degrees; set it on the fire, and when it boils, add an onion and a blade of powdered mace. Let it simmer gently for three-quarters of an hour; flavor the gravy with a tablespoon of mushroom or other catsup or sauce. Give one boil, and serve hot.

MISS ARMOR D. HEAD.

LIVER—FRIED.

Cut the liver in slices, not too thin, scald with boiling water, sprinkle with salt and pepper, dredge with flour or meal, and fry in hot fat.

BRAINS.

Scald and wash thoroughly, picking off all the membraneous substance. Parboil for several minutes, and drain; salt and pepper to taste. Put a little grease in frying pan; put in brains, stirring and mashing till they are nearly done, then pour in several well beaten eggs and scramble all together. Serve hot.

HASH.

Chop cold meat, an onion and a small Irish potato all together. Sift in a little flour, salt and pepper to taste. Put in a well greased frying pan and add enough water to cover. Cook till the water is consistency of gravy, and serve.

HASH WITH TOMATOES,

Brown two tablespoons of flour in one of lard, add a pint of water, a pound of chopped boiled meat, 3 tomatoes cut in small pieces or $\frac{1}{2}$ can of tomatoes, 2 small Irish potatoes chopped fine, salt and pepper to taste; also a half onion. Cook about an hour, adding more water if necessary.

MISS ELLA BEDELL.

VEAL CROQUETTES.

Chop very fine or grind pieces of cold veal and 1 small onion; place on the fire a half cup of milk, piece of butter the size of an walnut; cook this till it thickens, and stir into chopped veal; let cool. Roll into oblong balls, dip in beaten egg, then in cracker meal and fry a light brown. Chicken can be used in place of veal.

MRS. L. B. COPES.

PIG'S HEAD PIE.

Boil pig's head in salt water, and mince. Line a baking pan with rich crust, place meat in, season with stock, pepper and a dash of sage. Boil eggs, chopped fine, salt and stir in the pie. Place a crust on the top and bake brown.

MRS. LILLIE T. SHAVER.

BEEF STEAK PIE.

Line a baking dish with rich pastry. Place in this 1½ pounds of stewed steak which has been cut into small pieces, 3 or 4 slices of bacon, two hard boiled eggs sliced, ½ cup of butter, salt and pepper to taste. Pour in cupful of water, cover top with pastry, and bake.

Pork also makes a good rich pie.

OX TAIL STEW.

Take four ox tails, break at each joint in small pieces, put in a pot and cover with water; boil until tender. Add a can of tomatoes, 1 large onion, 1 chili pepper, 1 tablespoon of brown sugar and 1 of vinegar, 1 teaspoon each of cloves, allspice and cinnamon and a little salt. Stew for four hours or until meat falls off the bone.

MRS. S. B. CONWAY.

DUMPLINGS FOR STEW.

Two well beaten eggs, ½ glass of milk, 1 pint of flour or enough to make a stiff batter, pinch of salt, 2 teaspoons of baking powder; drop in the boiling stew and cook about 5 minutes, let cook 2½ minutes on one side and turn. When done, serve at once.

MISS BESSIE F. WALSH.

Entrees

A 1908 Austin post card that used five postcard views in miniature. From the top clockwise is the Capitol, Austin City Hall, the Main Building at the University, the Governor's Mansion and a view up Congress Avenue toward the Capitol.

ENTREES.

GRILLED ALMONDS.

Blanch a cupful of almonds; dry them thoroughly. Boil a cupful of sugar and a quarter of a cupful of water till it hairs, then throw in the almonds. Let them fry, as it were, in this syrup, stirring occasionally.

They will turn a faint yellow-brown before the sugar changes color; do not wait an instant once this change of color begins, or they will lose flavor; remove them from the fire, and stir them until the syrup has turned back to sugar and clings irregularly to the nuts. You will find them delicious to alternate at dinner with the salted almonds.

MRS. GEO. W. MASSIE.

SALTED PECANS.

Pick the pecans carefully, so as to have as large pieces as possible; put a small piece of butter in a shallow pan with enough salt to give a salty taste, melt it and put in the pecans; slip in a hot oven and let brown lightly, shaking the pan occasionally. Be careful not to get them too greasy. These are very nice, and some prefer them to the almonds.

SCALLOPED CHEESE.

Take three slices of bread well buttered, first cutting off the brown crust. Grate a quarter of a pound of any good cheese; lay the bread in a baking dish, sprinkle over it the grated cheese; salt and pepper to taste. Mix four well beaten eggs with three cups of milk, pour over the bread and cheese. Bake it in a hot oven until brown. This is nice for tea.

CHEESE FINGERS.

Roll out puff paste into a thin sheet. Brush over slightly with ice water. Cut in strips 5 inches long and 1 inch wide. Sprinkle over grated cheese. Bake in quick oven 15 minutes.

Victoria. MRS. R. L. DABNEY.

5—C. B.

CHEESE STRAWS.

Two cups grated cheese, ¾ cup of butter, 1 tablespoon of water; salt, cayenne or black pepper to taste; flour sufficient to make a dough. Roll thin and cut in long, narrow strips. This is excellent.

MISS EMILY TOBIN.

CHEESE STRAWS.

Two ounces flour, a little cayenne pepper, 3 ounces grated cheese, a little salt, yolks of 2 eggs. Mix all together, work in the eggs with the hands, roll out thin, cut in strips and bake quickly.

MISS ELLA FULMORE.

CHEESE STRAWS.

One-fourth pound flour, white of 1 egg beaten, ¼ pound grated cheese, 1 tablespoon of butter, salt to taste. Make up with ice water; roll out thin, cut in strips and bake.

MISS LOUISE SHELLEY.

CHEESE STRAWS.

One-fourth pound of flour, 2 ounces of butter, 2 ounces of grated Parnesian cheese, a pinch of salt and a pinch of cayenne pepper; mix into a paste with the yolk of an egg. Roll out to thickness of a silver knife, cut in strips ⅓ inch wide and twist them. Lay in a baking pan slightly floured. Bake in a moderate oven until crisp, but they must not brown.

BANANAS A LA CREOLE.

Take ripe bananas and slice them as one does cucumbers. Squeeze over them the juice of oranges or lemons, and sprinkle with sugar.

MRS. J. B. CLARK.

RICE SNOW BALLS.

One cup of rice, 1 teaspoon of salt, 1 pint of milk. Wash rice, let it boil with milk; add salt, boil till tender; put in cups in a cold place. When cold turn out on saucers, pour soft custard sauce around it. This is very dainty for children's parties.

Victoria.   MRS. R. L. DABNEY.

Salads
and
Slaw

The Capitol and the Austin skyline as seen from the University Main Building ca. 1907.

SALADS AND SLAW.

CHICKEN SALAD NO. 1.

To one chicken take 6 hard boiled eggs, chopped fine or cut if preferred; a bunch of celery, cut fine; a teaspoon each of mustard, pepper, salt, sugar and vinegar or pickle to taste; two tablespoons of salad dressing.

MRS. G. CROW.

CHICKEN SALAD NO. 2.

One grown chicken boiled very tender, when cool, mince fine; boil 6 eggs very hard and run through sieve; use either cabbage, potatoes, celery or lettuce. If cabbage, cut up fine; if potatoes, boil and mash; ½ teacup of chipped pickles; add black pepper, salt and 1 teaspoon of mustard.

DRESSING FOR SALAD.

One-half cup of strong vinegar, ½ cup of water, 1 tablespoon butter, 1 tablespoon sugar, 2 eggs beaten lightly; place on stove and boil, and when cool pour over salad; add sugar or vinegar, if necessary, to suit taste.

MRS. L. J. STOREY.

CHICKEN SALAD NO. 3.

Boil 3 chickens till tender, salting to taste; when cold, cut in small pieces and add twice the quantity of celery, cut fine. Four hard boiled eggs sliced and mixed thoroughly with other ingredients. For dressing, put on stove a sauce pan with one pint of vinegar and butter the size of an egg. Beat 2 or 3 eggs, 2 tablespoons of mustard, 1 of black pepper, 2 of sugar and 1 teaspoon of salt. When thoroughly beaten pour slowly into vinegar until it thickens; remove and pour over salad, add lemon juice to improve flavor, and garnish the top with slices of lemon.

MISS MARGARET CRISER.

POTATO SALAD.

Boil 3 or 4 large Irish potatoes; when cooked, cut into small squares; about half as much celery chopped up; cut 2 onions in small pieces; mix all together. Make a dressing of 1 teacup of cold water, 3 tablespoons of vinegar, 1 teaspoon of butter, salt and pepper to taste; put the dressing on the stove, cook until it boils; then add a paste made of a teaspoon of flour and 2 spoons of water. Mix until smooth before putting it into the dressing. Take the yolks of 2 eggs beaten well, pour the dressing into the eggs, stir well; put all back into the vessel in which the dressing was boiled. Steam for a few minutes, pour over salad when cool.

MRS. EDWARD ROBINSON.

POTATO SALAD (EXCELLENT) NO. 2.

Boil 1 quart Irish potatoes with jackets on; when cold, peel and slice thin. Slice 1 cucumber thin (or ¼ head of cabbage chopped fine). Six hard boiled eggs; add chopped whites. Smooth yolks with a teaspoon each of mustard, salt and pepper, tablespoon of melted butter; mix with potatoes, add 1 cup sweet cream and enough vinegar to suit taste.

MRS. C. H. LEBOLD.

POTATO SALAD NO. 3.

Peel and boil 8 Irish potatoes; cream well with 1 tablespoon of butter, salt and pepper to taste; 5 hard boiled eggs; chop the whites of eggs and 6 small pickles, smooth the yolks and 1 teaspoon mustard with a cup of vinegar. Add this, together with pickles and whites, to the creamed potatoes.

POTATO SALAD NO. 4.

One tablespoonful each of vinegar and water, 1 teaspoonful mustard, ½ teaspoonful salt, 1 egg slightly beaten, 1 teaspoonful each of minced onion and parsley; add a little cream to the dressing; 2 boiled potatoes, sliced thin.

MRS. JOHNSON.

OYSTER SALAD.

One large can of cove oysters, ½ teacup of vinegar, ½ cup of liquor from the oysters, ½ cup of crackers, ½ cup of butter, 1 teaspoonful of mustard, yellows of 4 eggs, 1 teaspoon of sugar; salt, pepper and celery seed to taste; mix. Put the vinegar and liquor on the stove and, when hot, stir in slowly the eggs, crackers, mustard and seasoning, which has been previously mixed. Pour over the oysters on a pretty salad bowl, and garnish with parsley and hard boiled eggs; then put on ice to cool.

San Angelo. Mrs. A. J. Baker.

SALMON SALAD.

One can of salmon; take out bones, and mash. Three hard boiled eggs; take the yolks, mash well, add a little pepper and salt, ½ teaspoon mustard and ⅔ cup of vinegar; pour over salmon; chop up the whites and 2 or 3 pickles, and stir in; put in salad bowl and decorate with yolks of 2 hard boiled eggs pressed through a sieve. The whites may be pressed through, too, in another part of sieve, or cut up with the others and put in the salad.

SALMON SALAD NO. 2.

Pour off the gravy to the salmon, and serve with mayonnaise.

APPLE SALAD.

Equal measure of tart, green apples and crisp white celery immediately taken from ice box. Mayonnaise dressing. The success of all salad largely depends on the ingredients being thoroughly chilled with ice.

Benedette B. Tobin.

TOMATO SALAD.

Take a box of gelatine, cover with water, let stand for half an hour. Take a can of tomatoes, put in stew pot; add a small onion, a little celery seed, salt and pepper; stew well, strain, and pour over gelatine. Pour into cups and let it set. When cold, turn into salad dish, and cover with mayonnaise. Put lettuce leaves or any green around edge of salad dish. This is a very pretty and tasty salad for winter when there are no fresh tomatoes.

BEEF SALAD.

Chop cold beef, cabbage and three hard boiled eggs; season well with mustard, salt, vinegar and pepper; add some pickles, chopped fine.

SARDINE SALAD.

One box of mustard sardines, boned and chopped fine with ½ dozen hard boiled eggs, 3 small cucumber pickles chopped fine, 1 tablespoonful of sugar, a little salt and vinegar to suit the taste.

MISS ELLA BEDELL.

SARDINE SALAD NO. 2.

One box sardines, 5 hard boiled eggs, 2 large pickles, 3 small Irish potatoes. Mix well together; add vinegar, salt and pepper to taste. Garnish top with hard boiled eggs.

MRS. LAURA McKEAN.

MAYONNAISE WITHOUT OLIVE OIL.

Yolks of 3 eggs, 1 tablespoon of sugar, 1 teaspoon made mustard, 1 teaspoon salt, 1 tumbler vinegar, 1 tablespoon butter; cook thoroughly, and this will keep for days. If too thick, thin with cream as you need it. This is a good way to use the yolks of eggs when making a white cake.

MRS. W. B. WORTHAM.

MAYONNAISE DRESSING NO. 1.

One pint of olive oil, 1 teaspoon of salt, 1 teaspoon of mustard, 2 or 3 lemons (juice), 2 eggs (yolks), a large pinch of red pepper. First have your oil, eggs, lemons and dish on ice, so as to be thoroughly chilled, then beat the yolks; when light add the salt, mustard and pepper, and then put 2 or 3 drops of oil and the same of lemon, beating hard all the time until the oil and lemon juice is all consumed; then put on ice, and let harden. The success of this depends very much on the beating.

MRS. EDWARD ROBINSON.

MAYONNAISE DRESSING NO. 2.

Yolks of 5 eggs, 2 teaspoons salt, 1 teaspoon dry mustard if for green salad, 3 tablespoons lemon juice, 3 tablespoons vinegar, 2 cups olive oil, ½ salt spoon cayenne pepper. Beat yolks until light; drop in oil very slowly at first, beating or stirring constantly until the mixture is like very thick cream. Add carefully other ingredients. The oil and eggs should be cold, when there is little danger of curdling.

These proportions are for five chickens, chopped coarsely, and mixed with an equal amount of celery. For potato salad use cold boiled potatoes cut into dice, instead of the chicken, adding to the dressing 10 drops of lemon juice.—*Chicago Cooking School.*

Recommended by Miss Louise Shelley.

MAYONNAISE DRESSING NO. 3.

Put the yolks of 4 fresh, raw eggs with 2 hard boiled ones into an ice cold bowl. Rub them as smooth as possible before introducing the oil. A good measure of oil is a full tablespoonful to each egg. All the art consists in putting the oil in by degrees. You can never make a good salad without taking plenty of time. When the oil is well mixed, having the appearance of jelly, put in 2 heaping teaspoonfuls of dry table salt, 1 of black pepper, 1 of mustard, cayenne pepper to taste (never put in salt and pepper before this stage or you cannot get your dressing smooth), the juice of 2 lemons, 1 tablespoon of vinegar. The mayonnaise should be the thickness of cream; if it looks like curdling while mixing, set in the ice box for half an hour and mix again. Put on ice till ready to be used, as it should never be mixed with salad until ready for use. This is my favorite recipe for mayonnaise for chicken salad.

BENEDETTE B. TOBIN.

GOOD MAYONNAISE DRESSING.

Put the yolks of 2 eggs in a deep dish with a little salt and white pepper; into these stir briskly some olive oil; add a few spoonfuls of vinegar. This dressing should have an agreeable flavor and rather stiff consistency. Salad oil should be kept well corked, in a dry cool place, and always in the dark.

MISS MARGARET CRISER.

SALAD DRESSING.

Beat up 2 eggs; add 2 tablespoons of sugar, piece of butter ½ size of an egg, 1 teaspoon of good mustard, a little white pepper, and lastly a teacup of good vinegar. Put all these ingredients into a porcelain sauce pan, and cook until thick. Cool slightly and beat in ½ cup of cream. This is good over any salad.

MRS. L. B. COPES.

CREAM SALAD DRESSING.

Yolks of 3 eggs beaten with 1 teaspoon of sugar, mustard, flour and pinch of red pepper. Heat 1 cup of vinegar and 1 tablespoon of butter; add slowly to the eggs, beating all the time; let cook a minute or so, when cold thin with sweet cream; add salt and vinegar to taste; whip until light, with egg-beater.

MRS. ORVILLE D. PARKER.

COLD SLAW.

One quart chopped cabbage; salt, pepper and sugar to taste. One cup of sweet cream, whipped. When stiff stir in the cabbage lightly; lastly add vinegar to taste.

MRS. C. H. LEBOLD.

CREAM SLAW.

One-half head of cabbage cut fine, $\frac{2}{3}$ cup of vinegar, $\frac{1}{2}$ cup of sugar, 2 eggs, and a piece of butter size of a walnut. Put vinegar, sugar and butter in a sauce pan, and let boil; stir the eggs, previously well mixed, into the vinegar and boil thoroughly. Then season cabbage with salt, pepper and mustard to taste.

DRESSING FOR LETTUCE OR SLAW.

Two eggs, well beaten; mix in 1 cup of olive oil or bacon juice, $\frac{1}{2}$ cup of vinegar, 1 tablespoonful of salt, a little pepper, 1 tablespoon of sugar, a little mustard if you like it; this will season 1 quart of cabbage.

Victoria.   MRS. R. L. DABNEY.

SLAW.

Chop a head of cabbage very fine and add salt, pepper and mustard to taste; and 1 tablespoonful of sugar. Take the yolks of 4 hard boiled eggs and mash smooth with $\frac{2}{3}$ cup of vinegar, pouring a little at a time. Pour this over cabbage, place in a glass dish, and cut the whites of the eggs over the top.

Vegetables and Side Dishes

A view of the Capitol from the Northwest in 1910. The old Travis County Courthouse is visible to the right.

VEGETABLES AND SIDE DISHES.

STUFFED CABBAGE.

Place a soft white cloth in an earthen bowl or small tin pan and strip the leaves from a nice sized cabbage head and line the bowl with layers of these. Put small slices of bacon and bits of sausage now and then between the cabbage leaves until all of the leaves are off, then tie the cloth together and drop into kettle of hot, salt water, and boil until done.

MRS. LILLIE T. SHAVER.

DRESSED CABBAGE.

One solid, medium sized, white head of cabbage; pour over this boiling water till the outside layer of leaves are withered, so you can turn them back without breaking them off. Cut out the inside and chop fine as for slaw; add to this about the same quantity of any cold meat you may have on hand, or a mixture of beef, chicken, pork and potted meat chopped; 6 or 8 hard boiled eggs; season with melted butter, pepper, salt and a little pickle if you like ; if too dry, moisten with warm water or stock; when well mixed place this back in the cabbage head, and fold leaves over it just as they were before inside of head was taken out; tie with a string and put in a cloth and tie tightly, drop in pot of boiling water to which a little salt has been added, boil till done, turn out whole on dish, garnish with hard boiled eggs, cut cabbage in slices and serve with drawn butter sauce, which is made as follows: One cup of butter, 2 dessertspoons of flour rubbed smoothly together; put into a sauce pan with a cup or two of water or stock, cover, and set in a larger vessel of boiling water; keep moving sauce pan; season with salt and pepper; when thick enough take off, cut up yellows of 3 hard boiled eggs and put in sauce. Capers are a nice addition.

MRS. JOHN ORR.

CABBAGE A LA CAULIFLOWER.

Cut the cabbage head into eighths, place in pot, cover with cold water, and let come to a boil; drain off water; recover with salted boiling water, cook until done, and serve with the following:

White sauce.—Rub together 1 tablespoon each of butter and flour; stir into a cupful of boiling milk, and season with salt and pepper.

CREAM CABBAGE.

Very much like cauliflower. Cut up a head of cabbage across the leaves as for slaw, put into boiling water with a little salt; keep covered closely; boil about 20 minutes or until quite tender, drain off water; add 1 cup of milk, piece of butter the size of an egg and 1 teaspoon of flour mixed in a little milk; let come to a boil, season with pepper, and serve at once.

MRS. L. B. COPES.

FRIED CABBAGE.

Chop cabbage fine, and salt; fry in one tablespoonful of lard, stir well; then add one pint of hot water, cover, and let cook down.

MRS. C. F. HILL.

CREAMED POTATOES.

Peel and slice, put on to boil in hot water; when they are done, pour off the water and let stand a few minutes covered, then shake well to make mealy. Mash well with potato masher; then add a tablespoon of butter, 1 teaspoon of salt and $\frac{1}{2}$ cup of sweet milk (to an ordinary dish full); beat well with a fork, till very light. Serve at once, as it ruins them to stand.

NEW POTATOES A LA CREME.

Take small new potatoes, throw in cold water, scrape, and boil in salt water till done; drain and add a cream dressing as follows: One dessertspoon of flour mixed smooth with a little milk, 1 tablespoon of butter and 1 cup of milk. Boil a few minutes.

POTATO PUFFS.

Two cupfuls of mashed potatoes; stir in 1 tablespoon of melted butter, beat to a cream; add 2 well beaten eggs, 1 cup of cream; pour in a deep pan, and bake till brown.

Victoria. MRS. R. L. DABNEY.

POTATOES FOR BREAKFAST.

Peel and slice them; boil a little; put a layer in a pan with a little butter, pepper, salt and a cup of milk. Sprinkle a little flour over the top, and bake till brown.

Victoria. MRS. R. L. DABNEY.

FLAKE POTATOES.

Boil potatoes with jackets on; when done, drain off water, wipe dry, and peel. Press through a sieve into a warm dish and serve at once. This is nice with fish.

CROQUETTES.

Take cold mashed potatoes, form in small flat cakes, flour and fry a deep brown in hot lard.

IRISH STEW.

Take scraps of cold roast and cover with salt water; add 2 or 3 Irish potatoes, sliced, and 1 onion, also sliced. When well done add a tablespoon of butter and a little pepper, and thicken with a tablespoon of flour smoothed with a little water.

POTATOES, DUCHESS.

Boil and pass through a sieve 6 fine potatoes; add 2 tablespoons of cream, yolks of 3 eggs, pepper, salt and a little chopped parsley, a hint of nutmeg. Mix thoroughly; take a tablespoonful at a time and form into balls; brush the top slightly with beaten egg; place in a buttered pan, and set in oven till nicely browned.

SCALLOPED POTATOES (KENTUCKY STYLE).

Peel and slice 5 or 6 raw potatoes thin as for frying; put into a baking dish a layer of bread crumbs, then a layer of potatoes with pepper, salt and small bits of butter. Continue this till all is used; then pour over the whole one cup of rich milk, bake until soft; if too dry, add a little more milk while cooking.

MRS. L. B. COPES.

SHOESTRING POTATOES.

Peel potatoes and place in cold water; cut in as fine strips as possible, and salt. Have a kettle of boiling lard; dry the potatoes on a clean cloth, and drop into the lard; when light brown take out with a skimmer and lay on brown paper till the grease is absorbed.

FRENCH FRIED POTATOES.

Peel and quarter medium sized Irish potatoes. Have a frying pan with plenty of boiling fat; drop in the potatoes, and fry a light brown. Let them get well done, then take out with a skimmer, and serve hot.

POTATO CHIPS.

Peel large potatoes, and put on ice. When cold slice thin with potato chipper. Put on the stove a deep frying pan nearly full of lard; when it is boiling hot, drop in the potatoes; as soon as they are light brown take out, lay on coarse brown paper so as to absorb the grease, and sprinkle with salt.

MRS. GEO. WALLING.

BAKED SWEET POTATOES.

Wash well, medium sized potatoes, and put in the oven and bake. If the potatoes are greased a little before baking they are more easily peeled. Some prefer boiling the potatoes till half done before baking.

CREAMED SWEET POTATOES.

Boil the potatoes with skins on till done. Remove the skins, and mash smooth; beat in ½ cup sugar, 1 large spoon of butter, and a cup of milk. Beat well and put in a deep pan, smooth the top with milk and place a small piece of butter on top, and brown in oven. One or two eggs added improves it.

MRS. SAM WEISIGER.

CANDIED YAMS.

Peel and cut in small strips two or three nice sweet potatoes. Boil in a little water till tender, then place in baking dish; add a spoon of butter, 1 cup of sugar and water enough to make a syrup. Bake in a moderate oven.

FRIED SWEET POTATOES.

Potatoes too large for baking can be used for this purpose. Peel and cut in slices ¼ inch in thickness, and sprinkle with salt. Have ready a frying pan with plenty of hot lard into which put the potatoes and cook slowly; it is better to cover them so as to get them thoroughly tender by the time they are brown.

STRING BEANS.

Into a pot of cold water put a good sized piece of bacon and let it begin to boil before putting in the beans, well washed and strung; add salt, and let boil till thoroughly done. Place on a flat dish and cut the bacon in thin slices over the top.

SPINACH.

Spinach requires thorough washing and picking. Put into boiling salt water and cook till tender. Take up on a flat dish, and lay over the top several poached eggs; pour drawn butter and pepper over the whole. Some prefer slices of hard boiled eggs for the top.

STEWED TOMATOES.

One can of tomatoes or a quart of fresh, peeled and sliced; add $\frac{1}{2}$ cup of water, if fresh. Stew till well done and add a little salt, and sweeten with $\frac{1}{2}$ cup of sugar. Some prefer them without sugar, but instead use a teaspoon of butter and pepper to taste. Before serving add cold bread broken into small pieces.

TOMATOES WITH MAYONNAISE.

Raw tomatoes peeled and served whole or in slices with mayonnaise is a pretty dish for luncheon or dinner.

STUFFED TOMATOES.

Cut a thin slice from the smooth end of several large tomatoes. Take out the center of each carefully. Fill the tomatoes with a mixture of bread crumbs, a tablespoon of butter, salt, pepper and the juice and inside pulp of the tomatoes. Put in a baking dish and bake slowly for three-quarters of an hour. Take up with a pancake turner and place on a flat dish, and garnish with sprigs of parsley.

MRS. SAM WEISIGER.

TOMATOES TO BROIL.

Take tomatoes, not very ripe, cut in thin slices; rub a little butter, salt and pepper together and spread over the slices, and broil in a gridiron or beef steak broiler. Serve hot.

MISS ARMOR HEAD.

A PRETTY DISH.

Alternate layers of tomatoes, sweet peppers and white onions, sliced thin, covered with crushed ice and served in a glass dish is pretty for lunch.

SCALLOPED TOMATOES.

Butter a pudding dish and put in alternate layers of tomatoes and bread crumbs; season well with butter, sugar, salt and pepper; dust the top with bread crumbs, and bake until brown in a moderate oven.

OKRA—HOW TO COOK.

Cut off both ends and put on in boiling salt water; drain off water, and season with butter and pepper.

MRS. A. A. HORN.

OKRA AND TOMATOES.

Take two slices of bacon, cut in small pieces, put in a stewpan and fry. Add a sliced onion and fry brown; next a quart of tomatoes which have been peeled and cut up, a quart of okra cut fine; cover the whole with water and boil slowly until well done. Season with salt and pepper, and just before taking from the stove mash with a potato masher.

MRS. ROBERT C. SHELLEY.

FRIED OKRA.

Cut up okra, roll in meal and fry in butter; season with salt and pepper.

BAKED ONIONS.

Boil large onions in plenty of salt water till tender. Butter a shallow dish and arrange onions in it. Sprinkle with pepper and salt, put a little butter in the center of each onion, and cover lightly with bread crumbs. Bake slowly, and serve with cream sauce.

CAULIFLOWER WITH CREAM SAUCE.

Take off the green leaves and stalk, and put on in boiling salt water. Boil for half an hour or until thoroughly done, drain; add 1 cup of milk, let it boil up. Thicken with 1 dessertspoon of flour rubbed smooth in a tablespoon of butter; pepper to taste.

EGG PLANT—VERY NICE.

Peel, slice and lay in salt water for 30 minutes, then parboil; season with pepper and salt; add ½ cup of milk, 1 egg, and 1 spoonful of melted butter. Put in a baking dish a layer of fine bread or cracker crumbs, then a layer of egg plant, and so on till all is used. Cover top with thick layer of crumbs; add a little beaten egg and milk; bake until nicely brown.

Mrs. L. B. Copes.

BAKED EGG PLANT.

Peel, slice and parboil one large or two small egg plants; when tender pour off water, mash, and beat in 3 eggs, 1 tablespoon of butter, half a cup of cream, 1 teacup of bread crumbs, 1 teaspoon of pepper, salt to taste, a small onion chopped fine. Bake in oven till brown.

Mrs. Pauline Drane.

FRIED EGG PLANT.

Peel, slice about $\frac{1}{4}$ inch thick, and parboil in salt water; when tender, dip in batter made as follows and fry brown: One egg beaten well, a little salt, 1 cup of sweet milk, 1 teaspoon baking powder and enough flour to make a rather stiff batter.

Mrs. E. G. Myers.

FRIED EGG PLANT NO. 2.

Peel, slice and parboil; when tender, mash with potato masher; beat in an egg, salt, $\frac{1}{2}$ cup of sweet milk and a teaspoon of baking powder, and drop a tablespoonful at a time in hot lard and let fry on both sides a deep brown.

BOILED ONIONS.

Peel onions and if they are large half them. Pour on boiling water to cover. Let boil till about half done, then pour off the water and pour on fresh boiling water; when done drain, and add a cup of milk, a tablespoon of butter, salt and pepper; thicken with a little flour made smooth with milk; let boil up again, and serve.

TO COOK BEETS.

Leave three or four inches of the top on to keep from bleeding. Boil till tender. Place in cold water and remove the skins with the hands. Slice and sprinkle with salt and sugar, then cover with vinegar, or, serve hot with butter and pepper.

FRIED CORN.

Shuck and silk tender corn (tie a little bunch of broom straws together and use for brushing out the silk). Have a sharp knife and barely cut the top off the grains, then scrape cob well; add a little cold water and salt. Put one tablespoonful of lard in frying pan and let it get smoking hot, then pour in the corn, cover and let cook till tender; stir occasionally to keep from scorching, and add 1 tablespoon of butter.

Mrs. A. A. Horn.

ASPARAGUS ON TOAST.

Boil in salted water until tender; drain. Have ready slices of dry toast, without crust, and place on each slice several stalks of the asparagus. Pour over the whole drawn butter and pepper.

BOILED ASPARAGUS.

Boil in salted water until tender, and then drain; add a little milk, 1 tablespoon of butter, and pepper to taste. Serve hot.

ENGLISH PEAS.

Boil green peas till tender, and drain. For every quart of peas add 2 tablespoons of butter, 1 of flour (smoothed in a paste), pepper, half a teaspoon of sugar, and 1 cup of sweet milk. Boil till it begins to thicken. Prepare canned peas in the same way.

OLD FASHIONED BAKED CASHAW.

Cut in half, scrape out the seed, put on bottom shelf of oven and bake till soft. Scrape out of the shell and season with butter, sugar and a little salt.

CANDIED CASHAW.

Cut in pieces and peel; cook till tender in boiling water. Then lay in baking dish and add 1 cup of sugar, a tablespoon of butter, a pinch of salt, and enough water to cover. Let it bake in oven till brown and the syrup is thick.

STUFFED PEPPERS.

Cut out the top and seed of sweet peppers. Take cold roast or hash meat and mince fine, a few cold biscuits crumbed in, salt, red and black pepper to taste, a lump of butter; mix all with meat broth, stuff in peppers, put in baking pan, sift a little flour over them, a lump of butter and some broth; bake until brown.

Mrs. D. H. Doom.

FRIED SQUASH.

When squash is young, don't peel it, but slice and parboil; when tender, drain off the water, mash and add salt and pepper. Put a few thin slices of bacon in a frying pan and fry out the fat, then put in a sliced onion and let brown, add the squash and let cook down.

SQUASH FRITTERS.

Cut up two medium sized squash, slice and parboil till tender; mash, and season with salt and pepper. Make a rather stiff batter with 1 cup of milk, 1 egg, flour to thicken, and half a teaspoon of baking powder. Mix in the squash, beat well, and fry in fritters to a light brown.

MRS. L. B. COPES.

LETTUCE.

Lettuce to be good must be crisp and fresh, and not bruised in cutting. Cut as fine as possible, add salt and sugar to taste. Boil 4 eggs hard. Mash the yolks, and add slowly, while stirring, a small cup of vinegar. Mix lightly with the lettuce and cut the whites over the top. It should be served soon after mixing.

MRS. SAM WEISIGER.

MACARONI.

Boil macaroni 25 minutes, then wash in cold water; cut it in short pieces, and add 1 cup of sweet milk and one egg well beaten, a little salt. Bake.

MRS. PATTIE DUNNINGTON.

MACARONI WITH CHEESE.

Break macaroni in short pieces and boil till tender, then salt. Place in baking dish alternate layers of macaroni and grated cheese and small pieces of butter; pour milk over it, and bake till light brown.

BAKED APPLES.

Take out the core of ½ dozen apples. Place in baking dish, cover with 1½ cups of sugar, a tablespoon of butter and water enough to keep from burning. Let cook slowly till apples are well done—adding water if necessary—and until the syrup is thick. Serve when cold.

6—C. B.

FRIED APPLES.

Cut with a sharp knife in thin slices, without peeling. Have ready a little pure sweet lard, very hot, in a frying pan; put in apples and fry carefully a nice brown. Add 1 tablespoon of butter and a half cup of sugar, and leave on fire till the sugar melts into a syrup. Peaches may be prepared in the same way and are very nice.

TURNIPS.

Peel and cut in thin slices across the grain, and lay in cold water. Put thin slices of bacon in a little water and, when it boils, add the turnips and boil till tender. Mash with potato masher and season with salt and pepper.

CUCUMBERS.

Lay cucumbers in cold water or ice box. Peel and slice very thin into a glass bowl. Sprinkle with pepper and salt, and pour over them a little white vinegar.

Pastry

Hood's Texas Brigade Monument was erected by surviving comrades and friends in 1910. The simple marble shaft is topped by a figure of a Confederate soldier. The monument cost $10,000 and was manufactured by the McNee Marble Company of Marietta, Georgia.

PASTRY.

All ingredients for pastry should be ice cold if possible. Don't work at all, barely mix so that it will stick together.

Pastry for all custard pies (where milk and eggs are used) should be baked a few minutes (not browned) before putting in the custard.

Pastry for rolls, dumplings, and meat pies, require much less lard than ordinary pastry.

It is a mistaken idea that meringue should be browned quickly. Brown slowly, giving it time to cook through, and it will not fall.

PASTRY.

Three cups of flour sifted with one teaspoonful of baking powder, then add one level teaspoonful of salt. Flake in lightly one cup of cold firm lard (or half butter, if preferred). Then mix in just enough ice water to put together. Don't work it at all, the larger the flakes the better.

PASTRY FOR MINCE MEAT.

Make up same proportion as above, roll out half-inch thick, spread with very yellow butter, then roll up; cut crosswise in pieces large enough for a pie, and roll thin. This is very pretty for the top crust of covered pies.

PUFF PASTE.

Take 1 pound of butter (be sure that it is of the best quality), free it from salt (by working it in water), form in a square lump, and place it in flour half an hour to harden. Sift 1 pound of flour in a bowl, mix up into dough with ice water; make as near the consistency of the butter as possible, so that the two will roll out evenly together. Now place the dough on the pastry board, dust it over and under with flour, roll out 12 inches long and 6 inches wide; then flour butter well and roll that out in a sheet about 8 inches long and 5 inches wide. Place this sheet of butter on the dough; you will notice there will be about one-fourth of the dough at the end and about ½ inch around the sides without butter.

Take ½ teaspoonful of cream of tartar, mix with 2 teaspoonfuls of flour and sprinkle evenly over the butter. Now fold the fourth not covered with butter over the butter, then fold the other part with the butter over that. You will then have 3 layers of dough and 2 of butter. Roll out to its original size, fold, dust with flour and roll again. Repeat the folding and rolling 12 times, placing the paste on a towel and then on ice between each rolling for 20 minutes.

When ready to bake roll out ¼ inch thick, cut with a very sharp cutter, turn upside down and cut about half way through.

This small cap can be lifted out after the shell has been baked. Before placing in the oven (which should be rather quick) brush over the top of each patty with the yolk of an egg beaten with an equal quantity of sweet milk, taking care not to allow any of it to run down on the edges, thus preventing the tartlets from rising fully.

Place them on a large, flat pan, allowing plenty of space between. When done take off the caps by raising them with a sharp pointed knife and scrape out inside.

When ready for use put in a moderate oven till thoroughly heated before filling with creamed oysters.

E. C.

MRS. TOBIN'S MINCE MEAT.

Four pounds of tender beef.
Three pounds of suet.
Three pounds of raisins.
Three pounds of currants.
Eight pounds of apples, chopped.
Six pounds of sugar.
One-half pound of candied orange peel.
One ounce of cinnamon.
One-fourth ounce of cloves.
One-fourth ounce of mace.
One-fourth ounce of allspice.
Two quarts of American brandy.

Boil the meat in salted water; when cold chop very fine. After removing every particle of membrane from the suet, chop fine. Mix thoroughly with the meat; salt sufficiently to remove fresh taste. To this add apples, then the sugar, fruit, spice and other ingredients; mix well, and cover close in stone jar.

MRS. BENEDETTE B. TOBIN.

MY MINCE MEAT RECIPE.

Three pounds of suet.

Six pounds of meat, heart and tongue.

Four pounds of raisins.

Four pounds of currants.

One pound of citron.

Six lemons.

Put on the stove and let come to a boil:

One quart of cider.

One quart of syrup.

One large or 4 small glasses of jelly.

Two pounds moist brown sugar, and spices to taste, nutmeg, cloves and cinnamon.

Pour this over the meat and allow it to cool; add 1 bottle of brandy, and pack in a stone jar (3 gallon for this quantity). Cover one-eighth of an inch thick with syrup. Add apples when you make the pies, as it keeps better without them.

If the meat is not moist enough when ready to use, add a little hot water and sweetened brandy.

A small lump of butter to each pie is an improvement.

MRS. JOHN ORR.

MINCE MEAT NO. 1.

Boil a round of beef until tender; when cold chop fine. To 1 pound of meat add:

One pound of suet, chopped fine.

Two tablespoons each of pulverized cloves, allspice, cinnamon, ginger and nutmeg.

One pound of brown sugar.

One pound of seeded raisins.

One pound of currants.

One pound of tart apples, chopped fine.

One pound of citron.

Mix well, put in stone jar, and cover with brandy.

It will keep all winter.

MRS. J. D. ROBERDEAU.

MINCE MEAT NO. 2.

Take a beef's tongue, boil and chop fine.

For one bowl of meat use two bowls of evaporated apples, cooked and chopped fine; two bowls of raisins and one of currants; ½ pound of citron, sliced fine; 1 pint of good vinegar; 1 cup of butter; 1½ pounds of sugar; cloves, cinnamon, pepper and salt to taste.

MISS FRANK SMITH.

TEMPERANCE MINCE MEAT.

Four pounds of lean beef.

Three pounds of suet.

Four pounds of chopped apples.

Two pounds of currants.

Two pounds of raisins.

One pound of citron.

Four pounds of brown sugar.

One lemon, chopped fine.

One-half teaspoonful of mace.

One teaspoonful of cinnamon.

One teaspoonful of allspice.

One teaspoonful of cloves.

One teaspoonful of salt.

Enough boiled sweet cider to cover.

Seed the raisins and use either chopped or whole.

MRS. NORVAL WILSON.

COCOANUT PIE.

Five eggs.

One cup of sugar.

Two cups of cocoanut.

One cup of milk.

One spoon of butter.

This will make three large pies.

LITTLE GEM COOK BOOK.

COCOANUT PIE.

Yolks of 8 eggs beaten well with ½ pound of sugar; set on the fire and add ½ pound of butter in small pieces. Stir till butter melts, remove from fire and stir in 1 wine glass of thick cream, 1 grated cocoanut. Bake in rich paste.

MRS. H. G. ASKEW.

LEMON PIE.

Make same as above, only use grated rind of 1 and juice of 3 lemons, instead of the cocoanut.

E. G. M.'S LEMON PIE.

Yolks of 6 eggs, beat well with
Two cups of sugar, add
One tablespoonful of butter.
One tablespoonful of flour.
Juice of two lemons, and 1 cup of sweet milk.

Line pans with rich pastry and bake slightly (not brown) before putting in the custard. Bake in moderate oven till jellied, then meringue with whites of 6 eggs and 6 heaping tablespoons of sugar. Cook slowly until light brown.

This is enough for three pies.

MRS. E. G. MYERS.

LEMON PIE.

One large cup of butter.
One and one-half tumblers of sugar.
Eight eggs, well beaten.
Three large lemons.

Cream butter and sugar light, add beaten yolks, then add grated rind and juice of lemons; lastly stir in well beaten whites. Bake in a rich crust in a moderate oven.

Bastrop.   MRS. WM. HIGGINS.

LEMON PIE.

One and one-half cups of sugar.
One cup of water.
Two tablespoonfuls of flour.
Four eggs.
One large or two small lemons.

Beat yolks of eggs very smooth; add the grated lemon peel and juice with the sugar. Stir in the flour and water, beat well, and pour into pie plates lined with rich paste.

When done, take from the oven and spread over thin the whites of the eggs, beaten smooth with 4 tablespoonfuls of sugar. Return to oven and brown slightly.

San Marcos.   MRS. GEO. T. McGEHEE.

OLD SOUTHERN LEMON PIE.

Juice of two lemons and grated rind of one.

Two cups of sugar.

Six eggs.

Small half cup of good butter.

One tablespoonful sifted corn meal.

Two-thirds cup of water.

Beat butter and sugar together, then add the beaten eggs and corn meal, water last. Bake in a rich crust. This makes two pies.

MRS. HATTIE C. COCHRAN.

SWEET POTATO PIES (GOOD).

One pint of boiled sweet potatoes, mash perfectly smooth.

One cup of butter.

One cup of sugar.

One cup of sweet milk.

Four eggs.

A little grated nutmeg.

Bake in a rich crust, and when done sprinkle with sugar.

MRS. E. G. MYERS.

SLICED POTATO PIE.

Line a deep baking pan with a rich paste, slice in some boiled sweet potatoes, cover plentifully with sugar and butter, and sprinkle with a little vinegar. Continue this till all the potatoes are used or the pan is nearly full. Let the top layer be the seasoning; pour on enough boiling water to cover, put on top crust, cut cross in the center and bake in a moderate oven.

CREAM PIE.

One cup of butter.

Two cups of sugar.

One cup of cream.

Five eggs.

Line pans with nice crust. Separate eggs, beat yolks well; add to this the cream, butter and 1 cup of sugar. Bake in moderate oven, and meringue with well beaten whites and 1 cup of sugar.

Lockhart.　　　　　MRS. J. T. STOREY.

CREAM PIE NO. 2.

One cup of sugar.

One-half cup of butter, creamed.

Two tablespoonfuls of flour.

Four eggs, well beaten.

Four cups of sweet milk.

Flavor to taste.

MRS. PATTIE DUNNINGTON.

APPLE CUSTARD PIE.

Three cups of stewed apples, green or evaporated. Sweeten to taste. Beat perfectly smooth; add

Three eggs.

One tablespoonful of butter.

One-half cup of sweet milk.

A little grated nutmeg or a few pieces of orange peel cooked with the apples.

Bake in one crust, and meringue.

JELLY CUSTARD.

Three eggs.

One cup of sugar.

One cup of jelly.

One tablespoonful of butter.

Lemon and spice to taste.

This must be baked with only one crust.

MOLASSES PIES.

Two cups of molasses.

One-half cup of sugar.

Three eggs.

One dessert spoonful of butter.

One dessert spoonful of flour.

One-half teaspoonful of soda.

One-half teaspoonful of vanilla.

Mix soda and molasses; set on the stove till it foams (don't boil), then mix in other ingredients. Bake crust slightly before pouring in the mixture. Bake in a moderate oven.

MRS. E. G. MYERS.

TRANSPARENT PIE.

Two teaspoonfuls of butter.

One cup of sugar, beaten to a cream.

Add yolks of 3 eggs and the beaten white of one. Bake with meringue. Bake crust first.

MISS KATHERINE DUNNINGTON.

CRANBERRY PIE.

Cook 1 quart of cranberries with 5 teacups of sugar and enough water to dissolve. When jellied take off and cool. Make rich crust and fill in with berries; put strips of pastry across the top or use meringue.

A VERY RICH DESSERT.

Take 1 large can of pears and 1½ cups of sugar, boil till syrup is thick.

Make a crisp pastry and bake in two layers. Over one crust pour half the pears, then lay on the other crust and add the rest. Serve with cream.

Any canned fruit may be used in the same manner.

PEACH COBBLER.

Stew nice firm peaches, stoned and quartered, and sweeten to taste.

Make rich pastry and bake in 'wo pans, the same size, being careful to bake brown and crisp without burning. When ready to serve, put together alternating pastry and fruit. Serve with sweetened cream and grated nutmeg.

MRS. GEO. WALLING.

CRAB LANTERNS, OR FRIED PIES.

Stew nice evaporated apples until well done, sweeten and spice to taste.

Make pastry, roll out in pieces the size of a saucer. Put one tablespoonful of the fruit near the center, fold the pastry over and round off the edges with a saucer. Press together with the fingers or print with a fork. Bake in a moderate oven until light brown, and serve cold with sweet milk.

In the winter these little pies are nice fried in hot lard and eaten warm.

STRAWBERRY SHORT CAKE.

Make rich pastry, bake in thin sheets in 2 tin biscuit pans. Bake crisp and brown, but do not burn.

When ready to serve spread on fresh strawberries that have been previously sweetened and mashed, having two layers of pastry and two of strawberries. Serve with sweetened cream, plain or whipped.

MRS. E. G. MYERS.

STRAWBERRY SHORT CAKE.

Make a rich biscuit dough, roll half and spread with butter; then roll the other half and place on the buttered half. Bake in a quick oven till brown. Then separate the two parts, butter them, and put a quart of strawberries sweetened to taste on the lower one. Cover with the other.

Serve with sweetened cream.

MRS. ROBT. SHELLEY.

STRAWBERRY SHORT CAKE.

One pint of flour (measured before sifting).

Two teaspoonfuls of baking powder.

Two tablespoonfuls of sugar.

Four tablespoonfuls of butter.

One teacup of milk, and a little salt.

Run the sugar, salt and baking powder with the flour through a sieve; then rub in the butter well, before adding the milk. Butter 2 tin pie pans, spread the batter in them, bake in a quick oven from 18 to 20 minutes.

Mash one quart of strawberries with $\frac{3}{4}$ cup of sugar.

Split cake and butter generously, putting half of the strawberries in each cake. Sprinkle powdered sugar on top.

MRS. ELTON PERRY.

ECLAIRS (CREAM PUFFS).

One cup of water.

One and one-half cups of flour.

One cup of butter.

One-half teaspoonful of salt.

Five eggs.

Boil the water, salt and butter together; when it boils, add quickly the flour; stir until it leaves the side of the pan. Add the eggs, one at a time, beating hard all the time, until all are used, then beat 5 minutes.

Bake the mixture in pieces 4 inches long and 1½ inches wide.

When cold split open and fill with cream; ice with chocolate frosting.

Filling: 1 pint of milk, 2½ tablespoons of corn starch, ¾ of a cup of sugar, 1 scant teaspoon of butter, 3 eggs well beaten. Wet the corn starch in cold milk, and cook in boiling milk 10 minutes.

Beat eggs and sugar together and add to the thickened milk. Cook 5 minutes longer, add the butter and, when cool, flavor with 1 teaspoonful of vanilla.

MISS ELLA F. FULMORE.

CREAM PUFFS.

One pint of boiling water.

One pint of flour.

One cup of butter.

Boil water and butter together, and add the flour, stirring until a thick paste.

Beat 3 eggs until stiff, stir quickly all together until thoroughly mixed. Place in the ice box. When ready, bake on buttered papers or tins. One tablespoonful for each puff. Fill in center of puff with whipped cream or flavored custard. This is a most excellent recipe.

MRS. BENEDETTE B. TOBIN.

BOILED BLACKBERRY ROLL.

(Apples or peaches are very nice, too.)

Make pastry, not too rich; roll out and spread with berries; roll up, pressing the ends together.

Have ready a pot of water boiling hard, dip in an old white cloth a little longer than the roll and wide enough to wrap twice around. Take out the cloth, sprinkle with flour on one side. Place roll carefully on floured side, roll up, tie the ends, and sew up the side. Don't roll too tight. Place in boiling water, cover and let boil rapidly about 1 hour. If necessary fill again with boiling water, as the roll should be entirely covered with boiling water till ready to serve. Cut off the cloth, slice crosswise, and serve with hard sauce.

BAKED APPLE ROLL.

Make roll as for blackberry roll, only use green apples, peeled and chopped fine. Place in granite or enamel pan (don't use tin), leaving room for sauce around the roll.

Put 2 cups of sugar, a little flour sifted on; $\frac{1}{2}$ cup of butter, or less, if scarce, and a little grated nutmeg or a few thin slices of lemon. Pour on boiling water, almost enough to cover, and bake in oven till roll is light brown, basting occasionally with sauce. If necessary add a little more water to sauce before serving.

Custards, Puddings and Sauces

Congress Avenue looking toward the Capitol ca. 1909. An intriguing picture of the past with the roof-mounted windmill, horse drawn carriages and electric streetcars.

CUSTARDS, PUDDINGS AND SAUCES.

BOILED CUSTARD NO. 1.

One glass of milk, 1 tablespoon sugar, and 1 egg to the person.

Bring the milk to a boil; then put in the well beaten whites of the eggs and scald; then take out. Beat the yolks and the sugar together thoroughly, and add the boiling milk; place on fire and as soon as it begins to thicken take off and cool. When cool flavor to taste; and in serving, place the scalded whites on top.

Austin. MRS. J. K. HOLLAND.

BOILED CUSTARD NO. 2.

One quart of milk, 4 eggs, $\frac{1}{2}$ cup of sugar, 1 teaspoonful of vanilla, 4 tablespoons of corn starch or 3 of flour. Put milk on to boil. Beat yolks of eggs with sugar; beat whites to a stiff froth; wet corn starch with a little milk (left out). Stir in boiling milk, then stir in the yolks and sugar. Cook until it begins to thicken; it is good to put the yolks in first with sugar, and when hot stir in whites. Then put in vanilla. Serve icy cold.

Victoria. MRS. R. L. DABNEY.

A NICE CUSTARD DESSERT.

Take a can of fine peaches or pears; drain off juice; chop the fruit and place in a baking dish. Make the following custard:

One quart milk.

Four eggs.

One cup sugar.

Three tablespoons corn starch.

Put milk on to boil; beat yolks with the sugar and corn starch; when the milk boils stir in the egg mixture, and cook until thick. Let this cool. Beat the whites stiff, and add a teaspoonful of sugar while beating, also a few drops of vanilla. Place the custard carefully over the chopped fruit, and set into the oven until slightly brown; now cover with the meringue of the whites, put into oven and brown. Let this cool, and eat with cream. It is better if chilled on ice.

MRS. L. B. COPES.

RICE CUSTARD.

To 2 cups of well-cooked rice add 2 eggs well beaten, 1 cup of sugar, ¼ cup of butter, 1 cup of milk, a handful of raisins or currants, and a little flavoring or grated nutmeg. Bake in a deep pan in moderate oven till light brown, but not watery.

BAKED CUSTARD.

(Good for the sick.)

Beat together 2 eggs and 2 tablespoons of sugar and 2 cups of sweet milk and a little grated nutmeg. Bake in small bowl till it solidifies.

Austin.   MRS. E. G. MYERS.

CHOCOLATE CUSTARD.

One quart sweet milk.

Four beaten eggs.

Five tablespoons grated chocolate.

One cup sugar.

Mix well, pour in custard cups. Set in a pan of water, and bake until done.

COTTAGE PUDDING.

Three tablespoons melted butter.

One cup sugar.

Two eggs, well beaten.

Two cups flour.

Two teaspoonfuls baking powder.

One cup sweet milk.

Bake in greased pudding dish, and serve with a rich sauce.

MRS. SAM WEISIGER.

CHOCOLATE PUDDING.

Let 1 pint of milk boil; add ½ cup of sugar, 3 tablespoons of grated chocolate, and 1 large spoonful corn starch. Boil until thick. Let it cool, and serve with sauce.

TEXAS COOK BOOK.

GRATED SWEET POTATO PUDDING.

Peel and grate sweet potatoes until you have about 2 cups. Add 1 cup sugar, 1 cup milk and ½ cup butter, flavoring and a pinch of salt. Bake slowly till brown. When cold, slice.

FRUIT PUDDING.

One and one-half cups of raisins.

One and one-half cups of molasses

Four cups of flour.

One teaspoonful yeast powder.

Flavor with brandy. Put in mold, and boil for 3 hours.

Sauce: Butter and sugar (creamed).

A most delicious dessert.

MRS. BENEDETTE B. TOBIN.

SOUFFLE PUDDING.

(For four people.)

Four eggs.

One cup milk.

Two tablespoonfuls sugar.

Two tablespoonfuls flour.

Two tablespoonfuls butter.

Cream the butter and flour together; place milk in porcelain sauce pan and heat to boiling. Then put in this creamed butter, and flour to thicken. Let this cool; then beat the yolks with the sugar, very light and add to the cooked mixture. This mixture must cool before the whites are added. Beat the whites very stiff; stir into the cooled pudding just before putting in the stove. Set in the oven and brown. Then this is to be served immediately, with the following sauce:

Two cups of sugar.

One-half cup of butter.

Yolks of 4 eggs, beaten light.

Mix these all together, place in double boiler, and stir until thick; add sherry wine or any preferred flavoring. Then beat the whites stiff, and whip into the sauce just before serving. This sauce is fine for all puddings.

Austin. MRS. L. B. COPES.

7—C. B.

QUEEN OF PUDDINGS.

One pint bread crumbs.

One cup sugar.

One quart sweet milk.

Yolks of 4 eggs.

Butter size of an egg.

Grated rind and juice of a lemon.

Put in stove until just done; then spread over top a thick layer of jelly or jam; then beat to a froth the whites, with a cup of sugar and a little lemon juice. Put in stove and brown a little.

In winter, to be eaten with wine sauce; in summer, made the evening before and eaten cold. Almost equal to ice cream.

Victoria. Mrs. R. L. Dabney.

GRAHAM PUDDING.

Mix well together ½ coffee cup of molasses, ¼ of a cup butter, 1 egg, ½ cup of milk, ½ teaspoon of pure soda, 1½ cups of good graham flour, 1 small teacup of raisins, spices to taste. Steam 4 hours, and serve with any sauce that may be preferred. This makes a showy as well as light and wholesome dessert, and has the merit of simplicity.

BURNT ALMOND PUDDING.

One cup blanched almonds.

One cup sugar.

One cup milk.

Yolks of 2 eggs.

One pint whipped cream.

One-half box gelatine.

One-half cup cold water.

Soak the gelatine 2 hours. After blanching the almonds, chop them very fine. Put 3 heaping tablespoons sugar in a pan, and, when melted, put in the nuts and stir until they are brown—about 4 minutes. Spread out to cool, and when cold pound them fine. Put them into the milk and boil 10 minutes. Beat the remainder of the sugar and eggs together until light; add the gelatine to the milk, stir until dissolved. Then add the eggs and sugar; boil until thick. Put out to cool; stir well, and add the whipped cream. Pour the mixture into a mould, put away and harden. Serve on a flat dish.

Miss Ella F. Fulmore.

BIRD'S NEST PUDDING.

Pare and core 6 apples.

Mix 1 pint of sour milk, 2½ cups of flour, ½ teaspoon of soda in a tablespoon of boiling water; mix all and pour over apples, and bake in a moderate oven 1 hour.

Serve with rich sauce.

Victoria.   MRS. R. L. DABNEY.

COCOANUT PUDDING.

One quart milk.

Two teaspoons (even) corn starch.

Three eggs.

One cup sugar.

One cup cocoanut, grated or dessicated.

One teaspoon butter.

Lemon extract.

Scald the milk. Stir in corn starch with 2 tablespoons of the milk (cold). Add the other ingredients, and bake in buttered pudding dish ½ hour.

EXCELLENT STEAMED PUDDING.

Two and one-half cups flour.

Salt spoon of salt.

Four well beaten eggs.

One cup brown sugar.

One-half cup dark molasses.

One cup sour milk.

One teaspoon soda.

Two tablespoons melted butter.

One cup seeded and chopped raisins.

One cup currants.

One-fourth pound citron.

Beat eggs well, add melted butter, sugar and molasses; put salt in flour, and soda into the milk. Mix all together and beat in the flour. Have fruit mixed and floured. After beating the batter thoroughly add fruit, with 1 teaspoon of cinnamon, 1 of cloves, and half of a grated nutmeg. Place in a steamer, and steam 3 hours. Keep the water under the steamer boiling hard. This is a fine dessert and will keep several days.

MRS. L. B. COPES.

POOR MAN'S PUDDING.

Soak stale bread; add ½ cup of flour and 2 eggs, raisins and pecans. Put in a cloth and boil two hours.   Serve with the following butter sauce:

One and one-half cups sugar.

Three tablespoons butter.

One-half cup milk.

One wine glass claret.

MISS LILLIE MELASKY.

BREAD PUDDING (WITH COCOANUT).

Two cups stale bread, grated, soaked in 1 quart sweet milk.

One cup sugar.

Yolks of 2 eggs, well beaten.

Butter the size of an egg.

One cup (dessicated) cocoanut.

Bake until done.

Beat the 2 whites to a froth and add a little sugar; spread this over the pudding, slip back in oven, and brown lightly.

This is to be eaten with sauce

MRS. SAM WEISIGER.

KISS PUDDING NO. 1.

(Nice, as a quick dessert.)

One quart sweet milk, 3 tablespoons corn starch, 1 cup sugar, yolks of 5 eggs, flavoring.   Boil the milk and stir in the starch, wet with cold milk; add the sugar and eggs and let it boil a few minutes. Make a frosting of the whites with a little more sugar, and brown in the oven.   Serve with rich cream.

MRS. JOHN ORR.

KISS PUDDING NO. 2

One egg.

One cup milk.

One tablespoon corn starch.

One tablespoon sugar.

Beat the yolk of egg thoroughly, to which add the sugar; moisten the starch and add to the boiling milk; add the beaten yolk and sugar, and let all boil until done.   Boil in a double boiler or it may scorch.   Beat vigorously for a few minutes and pour into a pudding dish, over which pour the beaten white to which has been added a tablespoon sugar. Return to the oven until brown, and serve cold with whipped cream to which has been added a little sugar. Flavor to taste. This will be enough for two people.

MRS. IDA HAGERTY.

LEMON SAUCE.

Mix 2 cups sugar, 2 tablespoons butter, 1 tablespoon flour, and enough water to dissolve; 1 lemon sliced thin, and boil till it thickens.

PRUNE WHIP.

Chop a cup of well cooked prunes, free from juice and seed; beat the whites of 5 eggs to a stiff froth and add $\frac{1}{2}$ cup sugar slowly while beating; stir in the prunes, turn in greased pudding dish, and bake in moderate oven till done. Serve with whipped cream or boiled custard.

BLUE GRASS PUDDING.

Five eggs, beaten separately.
One cup sugar.
One cup molasses.
One cup butter.
Three cups flour.
One cup buttermilk.
One pound chopped raisins.
One-fourth teaspoon soda.

Spice if desired. Grease the pan well, and steam $2\frac{1}{2}$ hours. Serve with lemon sauce.

SPONGE CAKE PUDDING.

See Sponge Cake.
Serve with sauce.

APPLE PLUM PUDDING.

Five large (chopped) apples.
One cup raisins.
One cup sugar.
One cup sweet milk.
One cup flour with 1 teaspoon baking powder.
One-half cup butter.
Two eggs.
Pinch of salt.
Bake 1 hour. Serve with any preferred sauce.

TAPIOCA PUDDING.

Beat the yolks of 4 eggs light; add 2 light cups of sugar, 1 cup of tapioca soaked over night, well drained. Let 1 quart of milk boil; then add the mixture, let boil until thick, pour over the beaten whites and stir in well; flavor with vanilla, and serve cold.

RICE PUDDING.

Boil 1 cup of rice in a pint of water, drain and add 1 pint of milk; stir in 2 ounces of butter and the yolks of 4 eggs with 1 cup of sugar; add the grated rind and juice of 1 lemon; bake ½ hour. Then beat the whites stiff and add 4 tablespoons of sugar; heap over the top, dust thickly with powdered sugar, brown and serve cold.

MISS ELLA BEDELL.

DELMONICO PUDDING.

Five tablespoons of corn starch.

One quart of milk.

Five eggs.

Six tablespoons of sugar.

Twenty drops of vanilla.

Mix corn starch with a little cold water, and just before the milk boils stir in the cornstarch with the yolks well beaten with the sugar. Make a meringue of the whites by beating them stiff, then stirring in 3 tablespoons of sugar.   Spread over the pudding and set in oven to brown a few minutes.

MRS. A. S. RUTHERFORD.

PLUM PUDDING.

Three cups of sugar.

One cup of butter.

One cup of milk.

Five cups of flour.

Seven eggs.

One teaspoon cinnamon.

One teaspoon allspice.

One-half teaspoon cloves.

Two teaspoons baking powder.

One ground nutmeg.

One and one-fourth pounds of seeded raisins.

One and one-fourth pounds of currants, cleaned.

Beat eggs, sugar and butter together.   Add flour, baking powder and milk, until the consistency of cake batter; then add fruit and spices. Have ready a bag of old strong cotton—seams turned out—about 16x10 inches. Wet with cold water, and flour carefully inside. Have ready a pot of boiling water, and in the bottom a plate; put the pudding in the bag, leaving about 4 inches for it to swell; boil constantly 4 or 5 hours; do not let it stop boiling; replenish with boiling water when needed; tear off the bag, and serve with hard sauce.

MRS. SARAH D. WALSH.

HARD SAUCE NO. 1.

Two cups of sugar.

One-half cup of butter.

One cup of thin, sweet cream.

Flavor with 2 tablespoons whiskey or brandy.

Stir together 1 cup of sugar and ½ cup of butter; add the other cup of sugar and the cup of cream, a little at a time, until all is well beaten and very light; flavor with the whiskey and grate a little nutmeg over the top.

MRS. D. H. WALSH.

HARD SAUCE NO. 2.

Cream 1 cup butter and 2 cups of sugar, and flavor to taste.

GOOD SAUCE.

One cup sugar and ½ cup butter beaten to a cream; 1 egg beaten well, ½ cup wine, 3 tablespoons water. Stir well and set it over a boiling teakettle a few minutes before serving.

VERY NICE SAUCE.

Beat the yolk of 1 egg with ½ cup of white sugar and a tablespoon of corn starch; stir in 3 tablespoons of boiling water; set it over teakettle to keep warm. Just as you take it to table stir lightly the white of egg beaten with other half cup of sugar, a little nutmeg and spoonful of brandy or wine.

CONFEDERATE SAUCE FOR CAKE.

Two cups sugar, 1 tablespoon of butter, yolk of 1 egg beaten well. Mix well and pour in ¼ of a pint of boiling milk; add a glass of wine, and season with nutmeg.

TEXAS COOK BOOK.

AMBER SAUCE.

Yolks of 5 eggs, 1 cup sugar, $\frac{1}{2}$ cup butter; beat all together very light, and add slowly 2 cups of boiling water. Flavor with 1 teaspoon cinnamon extract.

GOLDEN SAUCE.

One tablespoon flour mixed with 4 tablespoons sugar; stir with 2 cups milk. Cook and add yolks of 4 eggs, well beaten, and 1 teaspoon vanilla.

JOURNEAY.

CORNWELL'S,

THE

CORRECT DRUG STORE.

Prescriptions carefully prepared. Manufacturer of Fine Flavoring Extracts. Dealer in Choice Spices. Every article of guaranteed quality.

CORNWELL'S PHARMACY,
620 Congress Ave.

GOODS DELIVERED.   PHONE 288.

HYDE PARK WOODYARD,

Cheapest Wood in Town.

Quick Delivery.

Will give PREMIUM STAMPS where cash on delivery.

PHONE NO. 584,

HYDE PARK STORE.

Cakes

Two decorative postcards from before World War I featuring the Capitol Building.

CAKES.

~~~~~~~~

LOAF CAKE, LAYER CAKE, TEA CAKES, DOUGHNUTS AND JUMBLES.

~~~~~~~~

A FEW SUGGESTIONS FOR INEXPERIENCED CAKE MAKERS.

When directions for mixing the cake are not given, it will be safe to mix as follows: Cream butter and sugar well, next add beaten yolks (if the recipe calls for any), then alternately the milk and flour; sift baking powder, or cream of tartar and soda, with the flour. Lastly add well beaten whites and extracts.

In mixing angel food and sponge cake the flour should be added last, and beaten as little as possible; barely mix. All butter cakes should be well beaten, 50 or 100 strokes after the cake is mixed greatly improves it.

Measure all ingredients in the same sized cups.

Don't melt butter, but soften, if necessary, by putting in a warm place.

Eggs should be put on ice before using if possible. If ice is not convenient, a pinch of salt beaten into the whites will make them rise rapidly.

To insure good results, the best of everything must be used.

Too much baking powder ruins a cake.

Never grease a pan with butter, the salt in the butter makes it stick. Cake never sticks to a pan that is first greased, then dusted with flour.

All fruit used in cake should be dredged well with flour before mixing in the batter, to keep it from sinking to the bottom of the pan.

No cake should be baked in a very hot oven.

Take layer cake out of pan as soon as baked, but loaf cake may be inverted in a plate and left till cool. If it is hard to come out place a damp cloth on the bottom of the pan.

Cakes should be iced before they are quite cold, or, if not convenient to, dust flour over the top and the icing will stick better.

MRS. SAYERS' FRUIT CAKE.

Eggs, 10.

Butter, 1 pound.

Sugar, 1 pound.

Flour, 1 pound.

Raisins, 4 pounds.

Citron, 1½ pounds.

Figs, ½ pound.

Dates, ½ pound.

Almonds, 1 pound.

Orange and lemon peel, ½ pound.

Pecans, 2 cups.

Molasses, 1 cup.

Spice to taste.

Soak raisins over night in 1½ cups of whiskey. Do not dredge the fruit in flour, but add all the fruit to the raisins before making the cake. Bake 4 hours in a moderate oven. Line sides of pan.

This cake was first introduced into the Mansion by Mrs. J. W. Parker, of Taylor, and was used in the winter at all the receptions given there.

A GOOD FRUIT CAKE.

One pound of raisins (stoned and chopped).

One pound of currants (washed and picked).

One pound of brown sugar.

One pound of flour (browned in the stove).

One-half pound of citron (cut fine).

Three-fourths pound of butter.

Twelve eggs.

One cup of molasses.

One cup of chopped apples.

One cup of almonds (blanched and chopped).

One glass of good jelly.

Juice of 1 lemon.

Plenty of spices of all kinds.

Two teaspoonfuls of baking powder, and 1 glass of brandy.

San Marcos.   MRS. H. HARDY.

FRUIT CAKE (NO. 2).

One pound of flour.

One pound of sugar.

One pound of butter.

Twelve eggs.

Two pounds of raisins.

Two pounds of currants.

One pound of citron.

Two tablespoonfuls each of mace, cloves, allspice and cinnamon.

Two nutmegs (grated).

One tumbler of brandy.

One teaspoonful of soda.

Mrs. Z. T. Fulmore.

FRUIT CAKE (NO. 3).

One dozen eggs.

One pound of sugar.

One pound of flour.

Three-fourths pound of butter.

Three pounds of raisins.

Two pounds of currants.

One pound of citron.

One pound of almonds.

One pound of pecans.

One cup of molasses.

One tablespoonful each of ground cinnamon and cloves, one nutmeg (grated), one glass of brandy.   Bake 3 hours.

Mrs. Geo. Criser.

FRUIT CAKE (NO. 4).

One pound sifted flour.

One pound of sugar.

Three-fourths pound of butter.

Ten eggs.

Juice of 1 lemon.

A wine glass of brandy and 1 of wine.

Season highly with ground cloves, allspice, nutmeg and cinnamon.

Two pounds of raisins (stoned and chopped).

Two pounds of currants (picked and washed).

One pound of almonds (blanched and sliced small).

One cup of pecans (chopped).

After the batter is made, spices added, and before putting in the fruit, stir a teaspoonful of soda into a saucer of molasses and mix in the cake.   Then stir in the fruit (previously well floured) quickly and set to baking as soon as possible.   Bake slowly.

Waco.   MRS. BATTLE.

FRUIT CAKE (NO. 5).

One pound of butter.

One pound of brown sugar, creamed together.

One pound of flour.

Eight eggs, whites and yolks beaten separately.

Two tablespoonfuls of mace.

One tablespoonful each of cloves, cinnamon and spice.

Four grated nutmegs.

One glass of plum jelly.

One-half of a teaspoonful of soda dissolved in hot water.

One pound of candied cherries.

One pound of almonds (blanched and chopped).

One pound of citron (sliced).

One pound of pecans (chopped fine).

One pound of raisins (seeded and chopped).

One pound of currants.

One-half pound of dried figs (cut fine).

Lastly put in well beaten whites of 2 eggs.   Bake in a six-quart pan in a slow oven 6 hours.   Let stand over night in pan.

MRS. TEXAS CUMMINGS.

FRUIT CAKE (NO. 6).

One and one-half cups of butter.

Two and one-fourth cups of light brown sugar.

One quart of flour (measure before sifting).

Ten eggs, beaten separately.

One grated nutmeg.

One tablespoonful of ground mace.

Two pounds of raisins (seed and cut fine).

Two pounds of currants (cleaned well).

(Dredge all fruits well with flour.)

One pound of citron (sliced or chopped).

One pound of almonds (blanched and chopped).

One pound of pecans (chopped).

One gill of alcohol and 8 drops of oil of lemon.

Directions for mixing: Cream butter and sugar, add beaten yolks, then add whites beaten stiff, next add spices.   Lastly the alcohol and fruit, except citron, which place in two layers in the cake. Smooth over the top with water, and bake about 2 or 3 hours in a slow oven.   This makes one very large or two small cakes.

MRS. E. G. MYERS.

DRIED APPLE FRUIT CAKE.

Three cups of dried apples, put in soak over night, 3 cups of molasses.

Three and one-half cups of flour.

One cup of butter.

Two eggs.

One teaspoonful of cinnamon.

One-half teaspoonful of clover.

One nutmeg.

One teaspnful of soda in a little milk.

Two light teaspoonfuls of soda in the flour.

Chop the apples, put in the molasses, stew slowly one hour.   When luke warm stir in the butter; when cold the other ingredients.

Bake in deep dishes; is better in ten days after making, but is very good at first.

Victoria.

MRS. R. L. DABNEY.

VANITY CAKE (WHITE).

One-half cup of butter.

One and one-half cups of powdered sugar.

One-half cup of sweet milk.

One-half cup of corn starch.

One and one-half cups of flour.

One and one-half teaspoonfuls of baking powder.

Whites of 6 eggs.

Victoria.

MRS. R. L. DABNEY.

POUND CAKE.

One pound of butter.

One pound of sugar.

One pound of flour.

One dozen eggs.

Cream butter and sugar together, add a little flour then one egg, beat five minutes; add other eggs and flour in the same manner.

MRS. ANNIE P. NORTON.

OLD FASHIONED POUND CAKE.

One pound of butter and 1 pound of sugar beaten to a cream. One pound of eggs (9 or 10 according to size), beat separately. When yolks are well beaten, add to the creamed butter and sugar, beat again; lastly add whites. Flavor to taste. No baking powder is necessary if you have strength enough to beat very light. Bake in a moderate oven.

MRS. J. K. HOLLAND.

DRIED APPLE CAKE.

Soak 2 cups of dried apples over night; then boil in 2 cups of molasses for 2 hours. When cold, add to the following:

One cup of butter.
Two cups of brown sugar.
One-half cup of buttermilk.
Five cups of flour.
Five eggs.
Two teaspoonfuls of soda.
One tablespoonful of cinnamon.
One-half tablespoonful of allspice.
One cup of raisins.
One cup of currants, well floured.
Bake slowly for 3 hours.

MISS ELLA BEDELL.

SILVER CAKE.

The whites of 12 eggs.
Five cups of flour.
Three cups of sugar.
One and one-half cups of butter.
One cup of sweet milk, and a heaping teaspoonful of baking powder. Flavor with lemon extract.

MRS. ANNIE P. NORTON.

WHITE CAKE.

Whites of 10 eggs, beaten to a stiff froth; 2½ cups of white sugar, well creamed with 1 cup of butter; 3½ cups of flour; 2 teaspoonfuls of cream of tartar and 1 teaspoonful of soda; 1 cup of sweet milk. Mix the cream of tartar with the flour, and sift twice; mix the soda with the milk. Flavor to taste.

San Marcos.   MRS. GEO. T. McGEHEE.

WHITE CAKE.

Two-thirds cup of butter.

Two cups of sugar.

Two-thirds cup of sweet milk.

Three and one-half cups of flour.

One level tablespoon of baking powder.

Whites of 8 eggs.

One teaspoonful of vanilla.

Mix: Cream the butter, then add the sugar, beat thoroughly adding milk a little at a time. Then add flour and whites alternately. Put the baking powder in the last cup of flour, and after the cake is mixed add this last cup. Bake 1½ hours.

Contributed by

San Angelo.   Mrs. A. J. Baker.

GOBLET CAKE (WHITE).

(To be measured in a large goblet.)

Three-fourths goblet of butter.

Two goblets of sugar.

Two-thirds goblet of sweet milk.

Three goblets of flour.

One teaspoonful of baking powder.

Whites of 8 eggs.

Take one-half the flour and cream with butter; add baking powder to the other half of the flour, and sift in last thing with the milk. Beat whites to a stiff froth and add the sugar; put all together, beat well and flavor. Bake as loaf or layer cake.

Belton.   Mrs. M. H. Shanklin.

DAINTY WHITE CAKE.

One cup of butter.

Two cups of sugar.

Three cups of flour.

Whites of 14 eggs.

One teaspoonful of baking powder.

Flavor to taste.

No good cake can be made without thoroughly creaming the butter and sugar.

Mrs. S. L. Eldridge.

FINE WHITE CAKE.

Whites of 8 eggs, beaten stiff.

One cup of butter.

Two cups of sugar.

One cup of water.

Three and one half cups of flour (measure before sifting) with 2 teaspoonfuls of baking powder.

Beat butter and 1 cup of sugar to a cream, adding by degrees the water. Add the remaining cup of sugar to the beaten whites, then by degrees the flour and baking powder. Beat all together, 100 strokes.

MRS. L. B. COPES.

WHITE CAKE.

One cup of butter.

Two cups of sugar.

One cup of sweet milk.

Three and one-half cups of flour.

Two teaspoonfuls of baking powder.

Whites of 5 eggs.

One teaspoonful of lemon extract.

MRS. SAM HARLAN.

DAINTY CAKE (WHITE).

One cup of butter.

Two cups of sugar.

Three cups of flour.

One-half cup of sweet milk.

Whites of 6 eggs.

One heaping teaspoonful of baking powder.

Flavor to taste.

MRS. LILLIE T. SHAVER.

SNOWDRIFT CAKE.

One-half cup of butter.

Two cups of sugar.

One cup of sweet milk.

Three cups of sifted flour.

One heaping teaspoonful of baking powder.

Whites of 5 eggs.

Flavor to taste.

MRS. Z. T. FULMORE.

SILVER CAKE.

Whites of 16 eggs, beaten to a froth.

One pound of pulverized sugar ($2\frac{3}{4}$ cups), rolled and sifted.

Three-fourths of a pound of butter ($1\frac{3}{4}$ scant cups).

One pound of sifted flour (4 level cups).

Cream butter till light and white, add sugar and beat till well mixed, then add flour and whites alternately; 1 level teaspoonful of baking powder. Flavor to taste.

MRS. JOHN ORR.

PLAIN WHITE CAKE.

One-half cup of butter.

One cup of sugar, beaten to a cream.

Whites of 4 eggs, well beaten.

Two cups of flour, with a level teaspoonful of baking powder and $\frac{1}{2}$ cup of milk.

SNOW CAKE (GOOD).

One cup of butter.

Two cups of sugar.

Three cups of flour.

Whites of 6 eggs.

One-half cupful of corn starch.

One cup of sweet milk.

One teaspoonful of baking powder.

One teaspoonful of lemon extract.

Recommended by MRS. ASKEW.

SPICE CAKE.

One-half cup of sugar.

One-half cup of butter.

One-half cup of molasses.

One-half cup of sour milk.

Two cups of flour.

One-half teaspoonful of soda.

One teaspoonful of allspice.

One teaspoonful of cinnamon.

One-half teaspoonful of cloves.

Two teaspoonfuls of ginger.

Victoria.   MRS. R. L. DABNEY.

8—C. B.

GOLD CAKE.

One-half cup of butter.
One cup of sugar.
Two-thirds cup of sweet milk.
Two cups of flour.
Two level teaspoons of baking powder.
Yolks of 8 eggs.
Flavor to taste.

YELLOW LOAF CAKE.

Three-fourths of a cup of butter.
Two cups of sugar.
Three and one-half cups of flour.
One cup of milk.
Two teaspoonfuls of baking powder.
Yolks of 8 eggs.
Flavor with lemon or vanilla.

TEXAS COOK BOOK.

CHEAP CUP CAKE.

One-half cup of butter.
One cup of sugar.
One-half cup of milk.
Three eggs.
One and one-half cups of flour.
One teaspoonful of baking powder.
Flavor to taste.

CUP CAKE.

1–2–3–4 Cake.

One cup of butter.
Two cups of sugar.
Three cups of flour.
Four eggs, beaten separately.
One cup of sweet milk and 2 teaspoonfuls of baking powder.
Flavor to taste.

MRS. L. J. STOREY.

NOTE.—This is a splendid recipe for layer cakes and little cakes, to which may be added spices, fruit and nuts. It never fails.

MRS. E. G. M.

QUICK CAKE.

One cup of butter.

Two and one-half cups of sugar.

One cup of sweet milk.

Four cups of flour.

Three teaspoonfuls of baking powder.

Six eggs.

Cream butter and sugar; add milk and flour with baking powder. Lastly break in the eggs, one at a time, and beat well. Flavor to taste.

MRS. PAULINE DRANE.

MOUNTAIN CAKE.

One cup of butter.

Three cups of sugar, beat to a cream.

One cup of sweet milk.

Six eggs.

Four cups of flour.

One teaspoonful of baking powder.

Flavor to taste.

If you wish it especially white leave out the yolks and put the whites of 12 eggs.

MRS. JOHN ORR.

THREE EGG CAKE.

One-half of a cup of butter.

Two light cups of sugar.

One cup of sweet milk.

Three eggs, beaten separately.

Three level teaspoonfuls of baking powder.

Two and one-half cups of flour.

Flavor to taste.

MRS. L. J. STOREY.

SPICE CAKE.

Yolks of 6 eggs.

One-half cup of butter.

One cup of brown sugar.

One-half cup of milk.

One and one-half cups of flour.

One and one-half teaspoonfuls of baking powder.

Spice to taste.

MRS. Z. T. FULMORE.

PECAN CAKE.

One tablespoonful of butter.
Three cups of sugar.
Six eggs.
One-half of a cup of sweet milk.
Three cups of flour.
One teaspoonful of baking powder.
One tablespoonful of mixed spices.
One cup of whiskey.
Three pounds of pecans, chopped very fine.

MRS. GEO. ASH.

WALNUT CAKE.

Whites of 8 eggs.
One cup of butter.
Two cups of sugar.
One cup of milk.
Four cups of flour.
Two teaspoonfuls of baking powder.
Flavor to taste.   Nector or bitter almond is nice.
One pound of walnuts, chopped fine.

MRS. LAURA McKEAN.

WATERMELON CAKE.

White Part:
One cup of butter.
Two cups of sugar.
One cup of sweet milk.
Three cups of flour.
Two teaspoonfuls of baking powder.
Whites of 5 eggs.
Red Part:
One-third cup of butter.
One cup of red sugar sand.
One-third cup of sweet milk.
Two cups of flour.
Five yolks of eggs.
One-half pound of raisins, whole.
Two teaspoonfuls of baking powder.
It takes two persons to fill the pan, one to put the red batter around the center of the pan, the other the white on the outside.

PECAN LOAF CAKE.

One cup of butter.

Two cups of sugar.

Three cups of flour.

Two teaspoonfuls of baking powder.

One cup of sweet milk.

Whites of 8 eggs.

One teaspoonful of vanilla extract.

When well beaten, add 3 cups of finely chopped pecans. Bake in a moderate oven.

MARBLE CAKE.

One scant cup of butter.

Three cups of sugar.

Four cups of flour.

One cup of sweet milk.

One teaspoonful of baking powder.

Whites of 8 eggs.

Dark Part:

One cup of butter.

Two cups of brown sugar.

One cup of molasses.

One cup of sweet milk.

Four cups of flour.

One teaspoonful of baking powder.

Yolks of 8 eggs and 1 whole egg added.

Four teaspoonfuls each of ground cloves, cinnamon and nutmeg.

MRS. JOHN ORR.

CHOCOLATE LOAF CAKE.

One-fourth of a cake of bitter chocolate, grated; mix with 1 cup of milk, 1 egg and ½ cup of sugar; boil together and flavor with vanilla. While this cools prepare the following:

One-half cup of butter.

One cup of sugar.

One-half cup of sweet milk.

One whole egg and one extra yolk.

One teaspoonful of soda.

Two cups of flour.

Stir both mixtures together, and beat well. Bake in a moderate oven. Ice with chocolate icing.

MRS. L. B. COPES.

BLACK CHOCOLATE CAKE.

Two-thirds cup of butter.

Two cups of sugar.

One cup of milk.

Three cups of flour.

Two teaspoonfuls of baking powder.

Three eggs.

Melt ½ of a cake of chocolate, add a little milk to make smooth; add to cake batter after it is well beaten. Bake either as loaf or layer cake.

Filling for layer cake: Boiled icing mixed thickly with nuts.

MRS. ORVILLE D. PARKER.

WHITE MARBLE CAKE.

Whites of 6 eggs.

One cup of butter.

Two cups of sugar.

One cup of sweet milk.

Three cups of flour.

Two teaspoonfuls of baking powder.

Cream butter and sugar; add flour, then milk, and so on till all the milk is used, then the well beaten eggs; lastly a small quantity of flour with the baking powder. Flavor with lemon. Take out ¼ of the batter and add 1 teaspoonful each of ground mace, cinnamon and cloves and ½ of a cup of finely chipped citron. Drop in first a spoonful of white, then dark, till all the batter is used.

Lockhart.   MRS. J. L. STOREY.

HOW TO MARBLE CAKES.

Use any good white cake recipe. Take out a good cupful of the batter and mix with any of the following, according to the color you want: A little grated or melted chocolate; a few drops of fruit coloring in red, green, blue or almost any color; this is very harmless and a pretty way to make cakes when the color scheme is carried out.

Another way is to make a silver and gold loaf cake and take a cup of one kind to marble the other. Spice may be added to a cup of the gold batter and used to marble the white cake. When you have fixed the cup of batter to marble with, put into the pan about ⅓ of the white batter and then drop in half the cup of batter, in different places, with a spoon; put on another third of white batter, then drop in the rest from the cup; place the remaining third of the white batter on top, take a fork, stick into the batter to the bottom of the pan and draw fork out gradually, repeat 2 or 3 times (not too often) in different parts of the cake, and the results will be very pretty.

The same idea can be carried out for layer cakes, instead of using 1 cup of batter to marble with, use $\frac{1}{3}$ or $\frac{1}{2}$ of the batter.

CHOCOLATE LOAF CAKE.

One-fourth of a cake of bitter chocolate.

Four eggs.

Two cups of sugar.

One-half cup of butter.

One teaspoonful of soda.

Two teaspoonfuls of vanilla.

Mix chocolate, yolks of 2 eggs and $\frac{1}{2}$ cup of milk, 2 teaspoonfuls of vanilla, and put on stove to warm.

For batter:

Two eggs.

One-half cup of butter.

One-half cup of milk.

One cup of sugar.

One teaspoonful of soda dissolved in milk.

Three cups of flour.

Let the chocolate come to a boil, and when as thick as cream, stir into the batter, pouring slowly. Bake in a moderate oven.

For icing: One cup of sugar and the whites of 2 eggs, $\frac{1}{2}$ cup of water. Put sugar and water in a pan, and, when it candies, beat slowly into the beaten whites.

MISS BESSIE WALSH.

SOFT MOLASSES CAKE.

One-half cup of butter, $\frac{1}{2}$ cup of sugar, creamed; beat in 2 eggs, 1 cup of molasses, $\frac{1}{2}$ cup of sweet milk, 2 full cups of flour, 2 teaspoonfuls of baking powder. Bake in a biscuit pan in a moderate oven.

This makes a nice pudding by leaving out $\frac{1}{2}$ of the butter, and serving with sauce.

COFFEE CAKE.

Three eggs.

One cup of butter.

Two cups of sugar.

One cup of molasses.

One cup of cold coffee.

One teaspoonful each of soda, cinnamon, allspice, nutmeg.

One pound of raisins (stoned and chopped).

One cup of chopped pecans.

Five cups of sifted flour.

Bake slowly.

MRS. ORVILLE D. PARKER.

ANGELS' FOOD.

Whites of 11 eggs.

One and one-half tumblers of pulverized sugar.

One tumbler of flour.

One teaspoonful of cream of tartar.

One teaspoonful of vanilla.

Sift sugar four times, and flour seven times. Beat eggs very stiff, add sugar first, then flour and cream of tartar; lastly the extract. Bake 40 minutes in a moderate oven.

MRS. G. CROW.

ANGELS' FOOD (NO. 2).

Beat the whites of 11 eggs to a stiff froth; add to this 1 cup of flour, 1 cup of sugar, 1 teaspoonful of cream of tartar, having been sifted together several times; add 1 teaspoonful of vanilla; stir just enough to mix well. Put in a dry pan, and bake about 30 minutes. When done, turn pan down until cool before removing. After removing from pan scrape off the brown outside.

MISS ARMOR D. HEAD.

ANGELS' FOOD (NO. 3).

Whites of 11 eggs.

One tumbler of flour.

One tumbler of sugar.

One teaspoonful of cream of tartar.

Mix flour, sugar and cream of tartar together; sift 7 times. Beat whites and add slowly the other ingredients.

MRS. ANNIE P. NORTON.

ANGELS' FOOD (NO. 4).

Whites of 11 eggs, beaten stiff.

One and one-half goblets of sugar.

One goblet of flour.

Sift 3 times each. The third time you sift flour, put in $\frac{1}{2}$ of a teaspoonful of cream of tartar. Mix sugar into the whites first, then flour very lightly. Flavor with 1 teaspoonful of vanilla. Bake 40 minutes in a moderate oven, without opening the stove for the first 15 minutes.

Ice with $1\frac{1}{2}$ cups of sugar, enough water to wet; boil until nearly candy, stir slowly into the beaten whites of 2 eggs, add $1\frac{1}{2}$ cups of almonds (blanched and chopped). When cool spread thick on top and sides of cake.

MRS. THAD. C. BELL.

GOOD SPONGE CAKE.

Four eggs.

One cup of powdered sugar.

One cup of flour.

One teaspoonful of baking powder.

One and one-half tablespoonfuls of water.

One teaspoonful of lemon extract.

MRS. K. C. ESTILL.

VELVET SPONGE CAKE.

Six eggs, leaving out the whites of 2.

Two cups of sugar.

Two and one-half cups of flour.

One cup of boiling milk or water.

One teaspoonful of lemon extract.

Cream yolks and sugar together, add well beaten whites. Sift flour and 1 teaspoonful of baking powder 3 times, then stir in slowly, and very little. Bake cake in mold or layers. Ice with 3 whites and sugar.

ANOTHER SPONGE CAKE.

One teacupful of flour.

One teacupful of sugar.

One teaspoonful of cream of tartar.

One-quarter teaspoonful of soda.

Four eggs.

Victoria.

MRS. R. L. DABNEY.

SPONGE CAKE.

Ten eggs, beaten separately. Beat into yolks 1 pound of sugar and juice and grated rind of 1 lemon; then stir in whites, together with ½ pound of flour and 1 teaspoonful of baking powder. Flavor to taste. Bake in quick oven.

MRS. Z. T. FULMORE.

SPONGE CAKE NO. 2.

Three eggs, beaten separately. To the yolks add 1 cup of sugar, and beat well; next add 1 tablespoonful of water and the beaten whites. Lastly sift in 1 cup of flour and 1 teaspoon of baking powder. Mix in very lightly, don't beat. Bake at once in a moderate oven.

MRS. E. G. MYERS.

WHITE SPONGE CAKE.

One cup of powdered sugar.
One-half cup of flour.
One-half cup of corn starch.
One teaspoon of baking powder.
Sift all together into the whites of 8 eggs beaten to a stiff froth. Mix thoroughly; flavor with vanilla. Bake in square tins.

TEXAS COOK BOOK.

SUNSHINE CAKE.

Whites of 11 eggs.
One and one-half cups of sugar.
Yolks of 3 eggs.
One cup of unsifted flour.
One teaspoonful of vanilla.
One teaspoonful of cream of tartar.
Put cream of tartar into the flour and sift it. Beat whites to a *very* stiff froth; beat the yolks well and add them to the whites. Add sugar carefully; then the flavoring, and last the flour. Mix thoroughly, but lightly and quickly; turn into an ungreased pan, and bake in a moderate oven 45 minutes.

This cake is used at the Mansion, and has been a favorite a number of years at the White House.

MRS. JOS. D. SAYERS.

GOLD AND SILVER FIG CAKE.

Use any good recipe for gold and silver cake. Bake the silver cake in two long pie tins. Half fill a long pie tin with the gold cake batter; lay on it a pound of split figs, close together, dusted with flour. Cover with more batter till the tin is nearly full. Bake Put the layers together with frosting, the gold between the silver layers; and frost the top. If you have too much batter for the gold layer, make a small cake beside.

MRS. OWENS' COOK BOOK.

Any other fruit or nuts can be substituted for the figs.—MRS. E. G. M.

DEVIL'S FOOD.

One-half cup of butter.

Two cups of light brown sugar.

One-half cup of sour cream.

Two eggs.

Three cups of sifted flour.

One ounce of chocolate dissolved in one-quarter cup of boiling water; mix in batter.

One level teaspoonful of soda, mixed in sour cream.

Bake in three layers.

Filling: Two cups of brown sugar, $\frac{3}{4}$ cup of sweet milk, butter the size of an egg. Put on stove and stir till it comes to a boil, take off, whip till cool, and flavor with vanilla.

MRS. GEORGE WALLING.

DEVIL'S FOOD.

One-half cup of butter.

One cup of sugar.

One cup of milk.

Two and one-half cups of flour.

Two teaspoonfuls of baking powder.

One whole egg and one yolk.

One teaspoonful of vanilla.

One-half a cake bitter chocolate.

One cup of sugar.

One-half cup of milk.

Yolk of 1 egg.

Put this in a pan and set on the back of the stove; heat until chocolate is melted. Do not boil. Add to batter. Bake in layers, and put together with white frosting.

MISS ELLA BEDELL.

A DELICATE CAKE.

One-half of a cup of butter.

Two cups of sugar.

Three-fourths of a cup of sweet milk.

Three cups of flour.

Whites of 8 eggs.

One teaspoonful of cream of tartar.

One-half teaspoonful of soda.

Cream sugar and butter till light, adding gradually the milk, flour, beaten whites, etc. Bake in layers, leaving part of the cake dough to which add spices and a cup of raisins, stoned and chopped. Put the layers together. alternating the white and dark layers. Ice the cake when finished.

San Marcos.   MRS. HAMMET HARDY.

WHITE FRUIT CAKE (LAYER).

One cup butter.

Two cups sugar.

Three cups flour.

One cup water.

Whites of 6 eggs.

One teaspoonful of baking powder.

One teaspoonful of lemon extract.

One cup of chopped Sultana raisins.

One-half cup of citron, sliced.

One-half cup of almonds, pecans or cocoanut, whichever you happen to have.

Bake in layers; put together with boiled icing.

MRS. EDITH WEEDEN.

MARSHMALLOW CAKE.

Make cake same as above. Ice, and put sliced marshmallows between the layers. Flavor the icing with vanilla.

MISS ELLA BEDELL.

MARSHMALLOW CAKE.

One and one-half cups granulated sugar, 1 cup flour, each sifted 16 times, in the 8th sifting put in 1 level teaspoon of cream of tartar; beat the whites of 11 eggs to a stiff froth, add sugar to the eggs, then the flour. Flavor with vanilla. Bake in 3 sheets in a moderate oven. Put together with the marshmallow paste.

E. C.

MARSHMALLOW PASTE.

Boil ¾ cup of fine granulated sugar with ½ cup of sweet milk 6 minutes. Break in pieces ¼ pound of marshmallows, and melt in 2 tablespoonfuls of hot water. Place in a vessel of boiling water; stir until smooth. Combine the two mixtures and beat until thick enough to spread; add ½ teaspoonful of vanilla.

E. C.

CARAMEL CAKE—WITH RAISINS AND NUTS.

A light cup of butter.

Two cups of sugar.

One cup of sweet milk.

Three cups of flour (measure, then sift).

Two teaspoonfuls of baking powder.

One teaspoonful of vanilla.

Whites of 8 eggs.

Caramel: Put 2½ cups of white sugar into a hot frying pan, let cook till it lumps, a light brown color; then pour in a pint of boiling water. Let boil till lumps are dissolved. Then put in 1 tablespoonful of butter and 1 cup of sweet milk, and cook until the consistency of honey (better still, try a little in a saucer; beat with a spoon, if it creams it is done). When you spread the caramel on the layers, cover with chopped pecans and raisins.

Recommended by MRS. THAD C. BELL.

PECAN CARAMEL CAKE.

One cup of butter.

Two cups of sugar.

One cup of sweet milk.

Three cups of flour.

Two teaspoonfuls of baking powder.

Whites of 6 eggs.

Caramel filling:

Two cups of dark brown sugar.

One cup of rich cream.

Flavor with vanilla.

Cook until it drops like icing, then remove from the fire and pour 1½ cups of pecans in the caramel and spread quickly between layers.

MRS. L. P. SIEKER.

CARAMEL CAKE.

One cup of butter.
Two cups of sugar.
One cup of milk.
Three and one-half cups of flour.
Two teaspoonfuls of baking powder.
Whites of 7 eggs.
Flavor with vanilla.
Bake in 3 layers.

Filling: One cup of dark brown sugar, 1 cup of white sugar; cover it well with water, and let boil to candy that will break against a cup when you try it in cold water. Then add 2 tablespoonfuls of sweet cream and 1 heaping tablespoonful of butter. Beat very thoroughly in a cool place until thick enough to spread. Flavor with vanilla.

MRS. R. C. WALKER.

CARAMEL CAKE.

Use any good white cake recipe; bake in 3 layers an inch thick. Use the following filling: Two cups of very light brown sugar, if too brown it will curdle the cream; 1 cup of sweet cream; 2 tablespoonfuls of butter. Use a large cup for this measure. Mix, and boil until it threads; take off and beat until creamy; add a teaspoon of vanilla when it is ready to put between and over the cake.

"CHICAGO COOKING SCHOOL,"
Miss Louise Shelley.

PECAN CARAMEL CAKE.

One cup of butter.
Two cups of sugar.
One cup of sweet milk.
Three cups of flour.
Two level teaspoonfuls of baking powder.
Whites of 8 eggs.
One teaspoonful of vanilla.
One cup of chopped pecans (not too fine).

Cream butter and sugar; add milk and flour with baking powder, next the well beaten whites and vanilla, lastly the pecans. Beat well after mixing; bake in three layers in a moderate oven.

Caramel: Two cups of white sugar, $\frac{1}{2}$ cup of sweet milk, put on the stove to boil, at the same time have frying pan getting very hot. When the milk and sugar have boiled up several times pour 1 cup of white sugar into the hot frying pan, it will lump and brown; stir to keep from burning. When it has melted, and looks like sugar house molasses, pour slowly into boiled milk and sugar; stir constantly. If it happens to lump, put back on stove and cook till smooth. Add 1 tablespoonful of butter, 1 tablespoonful of vanilla and 1 cup of chopped pecans. Set in pan of cold water and stir occasionally; when cool, or thick enough, spread between layers and on top. Decorate the top with halves of pecans.

Mrs. E. G. Myers.

TUTTI FRUTTI CAKE.

Whites of 4 eggs.
One cup of butter.
Two cups of sugar.
One cup of milk.
Four cups of flour.
Two teaspoonfuls of baking powder.
Bake in 4 layers; ice between with boiled icing, and sprinkle on a thick layer of the following:
One grated cocoanut.
One pound of pecans, chopped.
One pound of dates, stoned and chopped.
It is easier to slice to make into two cakes of 2 layers each, having the filling as thick as the cake.

CHOCOLATE SPICE CAKE WITH NUT FILLING.

Three-fourths cup of butter.
One and one-half cups of sugar, beaten to a cream.
Three-fourths cup of sweet milk.
Four eggs.
Two and one-half cups of flour.
Two teaspoonfuls of baking powder.
One-half cake of sweet chocolate.
Spices and vanilla to taste.
Bake in layers.
Filling: Make icing and spread with chopped nuts between layers.
Taylor, Texas.   Mrs. J. Melasky.

MINNEHAHA CAKE.

Three-fourths of a cup of butter.

Two cups of sugar.

Three-fourths cup of milk.

Three and one-half cups of flour.

Whites of 7 eggs.

One scant teaspoonful of baking powder, sifted with flour 4 times.

Cream sugar and butter, adding milk, a little at a time, until all is used; then break in the whites of 2 eggs, add 1 cup of flour, stir well; repeat until all the eggs and flour are used. Flavor with lemons. Bake in layer pans.

Filling:

Three cups of sugar.

Whites of 3 eggs.

One cup of cold water.

One pint of seeded raisins.

One pint of picked pecans.

Put the sugar and water in a pan to boil. Chop the raisins and pecans together, and stir into the beaten whites of 3 eggs. When syrup is cooked to candy, stir in the fruit and eggs, and let cook a few minutes; put between layers. Ice the top and sides.

MISS BESSIE F. WALSH.

CHOCOLATE CAKE.

Use any good recipe for white or cup cake, and fill with boiled icing made as follows: Cook 2 cups of sugar with just enough water to mix, till it is almost candy. Pour slowly into the well beaten whites of 2 eggs, beaten until smooth, and add from $\frac{1}{2}$ to 1 cup of grated chocolate (according to how dark you like it). Flavor with vanilla, and when thick enough spread between layers.

This same recipe may be improved by adding a cup of cocoanut to the chocolate icing, or a cup of chopped nuts.

See Chocolate Filling in "Icing and Filling for Cakes."

ANOTHER GOOD CHOCOLATE CAKE.

Use any of the recipes for chocolate loaf cake; bake in layers, using all chocolate, or alternating with chocolate and white cake. Put together with any of the plain or chocolate icings, using your own taste about mixing nuts, fruit, etc.

MRS. E. G. MYERS.

BUTTERMILK CHOCOLATE CAKE.

Five eggs.
One cup of butter.
Two and one-half cups of sugar.
One cup of buttermilk.
Four cups of flour.
One teaspoonful of soda.
Three teaspoonfuls of vanilla.
Baker's chocolate enough to suit the taste and color.
Bake in deep jelly tins; put together with white icing.

MRS. LAURA McKEAN.

COCOANUT-CHOCOLATE CAKE.

One cup of butter.
Two cups of sugar.
One cup of milk.
Three cups of flour.
Two teaspoonfuls of baking powder.
Whites of 8 eggs, well beaten.
Bake in layers.

Grate 1 cocoanut. Make syrup of 2 cups of sugar, ½ cup of water, ½ cup of butter; let boil till thick, then put in cocoanut; let cook a few minutes.

Grate a cake of sweet chocolate; add half to the cocoanut and cook until the consistency of jam. Take from the fire, and when almost cold spread between layers. Make boiled icing; put in the rest of the chocolate, and ice the top and sides.

MRS. TEXAS CUMMINGS.

BANANA CAKE.

One-half cup of butter.
Two cups of sugar.
One cup of water.
Three cups of flour.
Two teaspoonfuls of baking powder.
Five eggs, leaving out whites of 2 for icing.

Icing: One pound of pulverized sugar, boiled with ½ cup of water, whites of 2 eggs, juice of half a lemon; after spreading icing on layers, put on sliced bananas and ice the top.

MRS. Z. T. FULMORE.

9—C. B.

COCOANUT CREAM CAKE.

One cup of butter.

Two cups of sugar.

One-half cup of sweet milk.

Three and one-half cups of flour.

One teaspoonful of baking powder.

Whites of 6 eggs.

Cream for filling:

One-half cup of sugar.

One-half cup of flour.

Whites of 2 eggs, beaten stiff; stir in sugar and flour; add ½ pint of boiling milk and 1 cup of good desiccated, or fresh cocoanut.

Make frosting for outside, and sprinkle thick with cocoanut before it is dry.

MRS. Z. T. FULMORE.

CREAM CAKE.

Yolks of 4 eggs, well beaten with 1½ cups of sugar.

One cup of flour (sifted 5 times).

One teaspoonful of lemon juice (not lemon extract).

One teaspoonful of cream of tartar.

Whites of 11 eggs, beaten dry.

Bake in layers.

Filling: Whip a pint of cream stiff; add sugar and flavor to taste. Fill cake and put in ice box till ready for use.

MRS. H. G. ASKEW.

ALMOND CREAM CAKE.

Whites of 11 eggs.

One and one-fourth tumblers of powdered sugar.

One tumbler of flour.

Two level teaspoonfuls of cream of tartar.

Sift sugar and flour 5 times. Cook in loaf, cut in half.

Filling:

One pound of almonds, blanched and chopped.

Whites of 2 eggs.

One pint of cream.

Whip cream and eggs; beat in sugar to taste; stir in almonds; spread between. Ice the top and sides.

MRS. LAURA McKEAN.

CREAM ALMOND CAKE.

Whites of 6 eggs.

One cup of butter.

Two cups of sugar.

One cup of sweet milk.

Three and one-half cups of flour.

Two teaspoonfuls of baking powder.

One teaspoonful of vanilla.

Filling for same:

Yolks of 2 eggs.

One cup of sweet cream.

One cup of sugar.

Two teaspoonfuls of vanilla.

One pound of almonds (blanched and chopped fine).

Beat the eggs, sugar and cream well together, and cook in a double boiler until thick. Flavor with vanilla, and then stir in the almonds. Spread between layers, and ice the top and sides with boiled icing.

MRS. WILL BOSWELL.

ORANGE CAKE.

Three-fourths cup of yellow butter.

Two cups of sugar.

Three cups of flour.

One teaspoonful of baking powder.

Yolks of 6 eggs.

Grated rind of 1, and juice of 2 oranges.

Bake in shallow pans; cut in squares or diamonds, and ice with boiled icing, flavored with orange juice.

MRS. EDITH WEEDEN.

CREAM CAKE.

Three eggs.

One coffee cup of granulated sugar, beaten together.

Two teaspoonfuls of cream of tartar.

One teaspoonful of soda, sifted with 1½ cups of flour.

Two tablespoonfuls of cold water.

Don't stir much after adding flour, just fold together. Split while warm and spread with the following filling.

Put powdered sugar on top.

Filling: Boil in a double boiler nearly a pint of sweet milk, with a good pinch of salt. Beat 2 small tablespoonfuls of corn starch with the milk; to this add 2 eggs beaten with 1 scant teacup of sugar. When nearly thick enough, add a piece of butter the size of an egg. Flavor highly with vanilla.   Stir constantly to prevent lumping.

MRS. ELTON PERRY.

TEA CAKES.

One cup of butter (or half lard).

Three cups of sugar.

Three eggs.

One cup of buttermilk.

One teaspoonful of soda in milk.

One teaspoon each of cinnamon and nutmeg.

Flour to roll stiff.

MRS. R. L. DABNEY.

GOOD TEA CAKES.

One cup of butter.

Two cups of sugar.

Two eggs.

Four tablespoonfuls of sweet milk or water.

One teaspoon vanilla or lemon.

Two teaspoons baking powder.

Flour enough to work stiff.

Roll out about ¼ inch thick, and bake in a moderate oven.

TEA CAKE.

Three-fourths of a cup of butter.

One and one-half cups of sugar.

Three eggs.

One tablespoonful of water.

One teaspoonful of extract.

One and one-half teaspoonfuls of baking powder.

Flour enough to roll thin.

Bake in greased pans in a hot oven.

MRS. EDITH WEEDEN.

ALMOND JUMBLES.

Blanch and chop (not too fine) ½ pound of almonds.

Cream ¼ pound of butter with ¼ pound of sugar.

Yolks of 2 eggs, 6 ounces of flour.

When well mixed add the beaten whites.   Roll very thin, cut with round cutter.   Bake a delicate brown.

MISS ELLA FULMORE.

NEW YORK COOKIES.

One cup of butter.
One cup of sugar.
One egg.
One-half a teaspoonful of soda dissolved in $\frac{1}{2}$ a cup of water.
Flavor with lemon.
Flour enough to roll soft.
Bake in a quick oven.

MRS. GEO. W. MASSIE.

CREAM COOKIES.

One cup of sour cream.
Two cups of sugar.
One egg.
One small teaspoonful of soda.
A little ground nutmeg or mace.
Flour enough to roll out (not too stiff).

MRS. R. L. DABNEY.

COCOANUT COOKIES.

One cup of butter.
Two cups of sugar.
Two eggs.
Six tablespoonfuls of milk.
One cocoanut (grated).
One level teaspoonful of salt.
Three teaspoonfuls of baking powder.
Flour enough to roll.

MRS. GEO. ASH.

GINGER SNAPS.

One cup of molasses.
One-half cup of butter.
One-half cup of sugar.
One-half cup of hot water.
One tablespoonful of ground ginger.
One-half tablespoonful of soda.
Two well beaten eggs.

Mix molasses, butter and sugar, and cream well; add the eggs; then by degrees the hot water with the soda dissolved in it. Enough flour to roll out stiff.

MRS. L. B. COPES.

GINGER NUTS.

One cup of butter.
One cup of brown sugar.
Two cups of molasses.
One teaspoonful of soda in ½ cup of hot water.
Two tablespoonfuls of ginger.
One teaspoonful of cloves.
Flour enough to roll.
Victoria.   MRS. R. L. DABNEY.

GINGER SNAPS.

Two cups molasses.
One cup sugar.
One-half cup lard.
One-half cup water.
A pinch of salt.
Two teaspoonfuls each of ginger, soda and baking powder.
Flour enough for a stiff dough.

GINGER SNAPS.

One cup of brown sugar.
One-half cup of molasses.
One and one-half cups of butter.
Two teaspoonfuls of soda.
Two teaspoonfuls of ginger.
Three pints of flour to begin with.
Rub shortening and sugar together into the flour; add enough
flour to work smooth.   Bake in a quick oven.
                                          MRS. WILL BOSWELL.

PEPPER NUTS, OR DUTCH COOKIES.

One pound of sugar and 4 eggs beaten well together; 1 teaspoonful
each of cinnamon, cloves, allspice and 1 nutmeg (grated).
One-half pound of citron and a soup plate full of pecans (chop-
ped).
One wine glass of whiskey.
One pound of flour, 1 teaspoonful of baking powder.
Mix well, roll out, cut in small cakes and bake in a hot oven.
                                          MRS. W. W. HARRIS.

LEP CAKE.

One and one-fourth cups of dark molasses, same amount of sugar, 1 cake of sweet chocolate (grated).

Six eggs, leave out whites of two for icing.

One cup of raisins (stoned and chopped).

One cup of citron, sliced.

Two cups of pecans, chopped.

Spices to taste.

Three and one-half cups of flour.

Two teaspoonfuls of baking powder.

One cup of brandy.

Bake in thin layers, in baking pan, cut in squares and ice.

Taylor.   MRS. J. MELASKY.

LEP CAKE NO. 2.

One cup of butter.

Two cups of sugar.

Three cups of flour.

Two teaspoonfuls of baking powder.

One cup of water.

Four eggs.

One-half ounce of bitter chocolate, melted and poured in the batter.

One and one-half cups of raisins (stoned and chopped).

One-fourth pound of citron, sliced (or any kind of fruit and nuts you may happen to have).

One teaspoonful of cinnamon.

One-half teaspoonful of cloves.

Bake in muffin pans, and ice with plain icing.

MRS. EDITH WEEDEN.

PECAN CAKES.

One cup of sugar.

One cup of flour.

Three eggs.

One cup of pecans.

One-half cake of chocolate.

One teaspoonful of baking powder.

Bake in buttered tins.

MISS LILLIE MELASKY.

GINGER SNAPS.

Rub 1 pound of butter into 2½ pounds of flour; add ½ pound brown sugar, tablespoonful of ground ginger, pinch of salt, dash of ground cayenne; mix well, add 1 pint sugarhouse molasses; flour enough to roll thin. Cut with a small cutter, and bake in a moderate oven till light brown.

MRS. D. H. DOOM.

PECAN COOKIES.

One cup of butter.

Two cups of sugar.

One-half cup of sweet milk.

Four eggs, well beaten.

One heaping cup of pecans, chopped.

Mix pecans with sugar and eggs, enough flour to mix and roll thin. Baking powder and extract.

MRS. L. P. SIEKER.

BROT TARTS.

Yolks of 10 eggs, beat well with 1 pound of granulated sugar.

Two cups of grated rye bread, well sifted.

One cake of sweet chocolate.

Ten cents worth of almonds.

Five cents worth of citron.

Ten cents worth of figs.

Two lemons, grated rind and juice.

One teaspoon each of cloves and cinnamon.

One wine glass of whiskey.

Whites of 10 eggs.

Two teaspoonfuls of baking powder.

Mix bread, chocolate, nuts, fruit and spice.

Then lemon is grated in the eggs and sugar.

Very fine.

MISS LILLIE MELASKY.

LOVE.

Beat the yolks of 2 eggs, add a pinch of salt, then work in flour slowly until it is too stiff to work in another ounce. Break in bits the size of a walnut, and roll till thin as paper. Fry in boiling hot lard and sprinkle with powdered sugar.

Nice to eat with chocolate.

MISS BELLE CHAPMAN.

GRAHAM CRACKERS.

One cup of sugar.
One cup of sour milk.
One cup of butter.
One teaspoonful of soda.
Thicken quite stiff with graham flour, and roll very thin.

Mrs. W. B. Wortham.

WAFERS.

One cup of butter.
Two cups of sugar.
One-half cup of sweet milk.
Three eggs.
Two heaping teaspoonfuls of baking powder.
Flavor to taste.   Flour enough to roll thin.   Mix as for cake.
Victoria.   Mrs. R. L. Dabney.

DOMINOES.

Use any good cup cake recipe; pour in greased shallow pans to the depth of ½ inch.   When done turn out on cloth, cut in oblong pieces the shape of dominoes, only larger, ice with white icing.   Take a little of the icing, mix with chocolate, put in a paper tube, and make dots and lines like dominoes.

Mrs. R. L. Dabney.

1-2-3-4 JUMBLES.

One cup of butter.
Two cups of sugar.
Three cups of flour.
Four eggs.
Mix in usual manner.   Drop from a spoon on a hot greased pan, about 2 inches apart, and bake in a hot oven.

Mrs. Owen's Cook Book.

LADY FINGERS.

Three eggs.
Three tablespoonfuls of sugar.
Three tablespoonfuls of flour.
One teaspoon of lemon or vanilla.
Cream yolks and sugar, add flour and baking powder.   Last add whites, well beaten.   Squeeze through a paper funnel onto a greased biscuit pan, and bake in a hot oven.

NONDESCRIPTS.

Beat the yolks of 5 eggs; add flour enough to make a dough. Roll very thin, and fry in boiling lard. When done sift powdered sugar over them.

MRS. K. C. ESTILL.

DOUGHNUTS.

Two eggs, beaten separately.
One teaspoonful of butter.
One-half cup of sweet milk.
One cup of sugar.
One teaspoonful of baking powder.
Flour enough to roll thin.

Cut in long narrow strips, join the ends and fry in boiling lard. Powder with sugar.

CRULLERS.

One and one-half cups of sugar.
One heaping teaspoonful of butter.
Two eggs.
Three-fourths cup of sour milk.
One-fourth teaspoonful of soda.
One level teaspoonful of baking powder.
Flour enough to roll.

Cut in small pieces, and fry in a plenty of boiling lard.

MRS. EDITH WEEDEN.

CRULLERS.

Three eggs.
Two coffee cups of sugar.
Not quite a cup of milk.
One tablespoonful of butter.
Three teaspoonfuls of baking powder mixed with 6 cups of flour.
One-half a nutmeg, grated.
One teaspoonful of ground cinnamon.

Beat eggs, sugar and butter together; add milk and spices. Roll thin, cut in squares, fry in hot lard, dust with powdered sugar.

MRS. LAURA McKEAN.

Icing and Filling for Cakes

Looking South from the Capitol in 1911. The Travis County Court House is at the left and in the distance on the left is the Littlefield Building and on the right, the Scarbrough Building.

ICING AND FILLING FOR CAKES.

BOILED ICING.

Two cups of white sugar.

One-half cup of water, boiled until it will click in cold water.

Pour slowly into the well beaten whites of 2 eggs; beat constantly; flavor, and whip till it is thick enough to spread.

This is enough to ice a large cake; it can be halved or doubled according to the amount desired.

Victoria.   Mrs. R. L. Dabney.

COLD FROSTING.

Beat white of 1 or 2 eggs, then stir in all the pulverized sugar it will take, flavor and beat well till smooth; then spread on cake.

GOLD FROSTING.

Yolks of 2 eggs, beaten well with 1 cup of sugar. Flavor with orange juice or vanilla.

CHOCOLATE ICING.

Use recipe for boiled icing, and, when beaten smooth, grate in enough chocolate to make the desired color.

CHOCOLATE FILLING.

Two cups of sugar wet with sweet milk. Grate in chocolate to suit taste. Boil till thick, then put in a large lump of butter; remove from stove, and stir till thick enough to spread on the cake.

Mrs. S. P. Weisiger.

CHOCOLATE FILLING NO. 2.

One egg.

One cup of sugar.

One-half cup of chocolate.

Flavor with vanilla.

Cook in double boiler till thick and smooth. Stir to prevent lumping. Double the recipe if a larger amount is required.

CHOCOLATE FILLING WITH NUTS.

A cup of grated cocoanut or any chopped nuts added to the above chocolate recipes improves the taste, especially in winter when rich cakes are used.

CARAMEL FILLING.

Two-cups of brown sugar.

One-half cup of cream or milk.

A piece of butter the size of an egg, or a larger piece if milk is used. Flavor with vanilla.

Cook until it becomes hard, put a little on a spoon and try in cold water.   Stir the mixture constantly.

MRS. W. R. HAMBY.

CREAM AND CHOCOLATE CARAMEL.

One cup of sweet cream.

Two cups of white sugar.

One tablespoonful of butter.

Boil until thick as cream, stirring constantly.

Remove from fire and stir until cold.

For chocolate caramel add to the above as much chocolate as desired.

Waco.   MRS. BATTLE.

COCOANUT FILLING.

Make boiled icing according to recipe, and, when it is beaten smooth, beat in a grated cocoanut, keeping out about a half of a cupful to sprinkle over the cake.

MARSHMALLOW FILLING.

One-half pound of fresh marshmallows melted, but not browned; then beat into boiled icing.   Flavor.   Spread thickly between layers.

LEMON JELLY.

Two cups of sugar

Two eggs, beat well together.

One tablespoonful of butter.

One tablespoonful of flour.

Juice of 2 lemons.

Cook over boiling water until it thickens.

LEMON FILLING.

The grated rind and juice of two lemons, the yolks of three eggs, beaten light, one cup of sugar, a lump of butter the size of a walnut mixed with one teaspoonful of flour. Cook on a slow fire, stirring until thick; lastly add the beaten whites of two eggs.

LITTLE GEM COOK BOOK.

FILLING FOR CREAM CAKE OR PUFFS.

One cup of sugar.
Two eggs.
One-half cup of flour.
One pint of sweet milk.
Cook until thick, flavor to taste.

FILLING FOR CREAM CAKE.

One cup of milk, when boiling add one egg.
Two tablespoonfuls of sugar.
One heaping teaspoonful of flour, beaten well together.
Stir until it boils. When cool flavor with one teaspoonful of vanilla or lemon.

VANITY CREAM.

One cup of jelly.
One cup of sugar, mixed with beaten white of one egg, beat all until stiff, spread between layers.

MALAGA FROSTING.

Beat a cup of stoned and chopped raisins into boiled icing.

PINEAPPLE FILLING.

Ice cakes with boiled icing when it is nearly cold. Drain juice from a can of grated pineapple, put a few spoons full of pineapple on the icing, then spread on more icing.

In this way the cake may be kept a few days without getting soggy.

Ice Cream,
Sherbet,
Ices,
Punches

An early view from the Capitol dome looking Southeast. At the left is the General Land Office building. On the far right is an edge of the Travis County Courthouse. The Jailor's residence and the County Jail are just to the east of the Courthouse. At the center is the Methodist Church facing St. Mary's Catholic Church.

ICE CREAM, SHERBET, ICES, PUNCHES

FROZEN AND CONGEALED DESSERTS.

One tablespoon of gelatine or corn starch dissolved and added to any water ice will make it easier to freeze.

ICE CREAM NO. 1.

One pint of sweet cream, ¼ of a box of gelatine dissolved in cold water, whites of 2 eggs beaten stiff; add sugar to taste. Flavor with vanilla. Freeze.

MRS. PAULINE DRANE.

ICE CREAM NO. 2.

Six goblets sweet milk, put on stove; beat together 6 eggs and 6 tablespoons sugar; when the milk boils, pour slowly over the well beaten eggs and sugar, stirring constantly; put back on the stove and stir till it thickens, being careful to take off before it curdles. When cool stir in 1 quart of sweet cream, sweetened to taste; flavor and freeze.

If fruit is added, sweeten and put in when cream is about half frozen.

MRS. E. G. MYERS.

SPANISH CREAM.

Dissolve ½ box of gelatine in 1 pint of milk; when thoroughly dissolved boil, and add the yolks of 2 eggs, beaten with ½ teacup of sugar. When it comes to a boil, remove from the fire, add the whites of the eggs, beaten to a froth; flavor to taste, and freeze.

MRS. J. D. ROBERDEAU.

SHERRY ICE CREAM.

One pint of new milk.

One quart of cream.

Two eggs.

One-half coffee cup of sugar.

One-half coffee cup of sherry.

One-half coffee cup of raisins, seeded and quartered.

Put the milk and sugar in a double boiler to heat, and stir until dissolved. Beat the eggs until creamy and strain them into the milk through a fine wire sieve. Let cook a few moments without boiling, and set off to cool. Pour the sherry over the raisins several hours before using. When the milk, eggs and sugar are cool, add the raisins, cream and sherry; and freeze.

San Angelo.   MRS. A. J. BAKER.

CARAMEL ICE CREAM.

Two quarts of milk, 5 eggs, sweeten to taste with maple syrup; make into a custard; when cold, add 1 quart of cream; flavor with vanilla, but it has more of a maple flavor to leave vanilla out. Freeze.

MRS. LAURA McKEAN.

MARASCHINO ICE CREAM.

Make 2 quarts of any good plain cream. When partly frozen add half a bottle of Maraschino cherries, chopped fine, with their juices.

MRS. H. B. HOUSTON.

APRICOT ICE CREAM.

One quart fresh milk, 1 quart cream. Large can best apricots; sweeten to taste; run apricots through thin cloth, so no skins will be in cream; freeze—can be made in fifteen minutes.

MRS. LAURA McKEAN.

MILK SHERBET.

One quart rich milk, 2 cups sugar. Put in freezer and when halfway frozen add juice of 4 lemons. Turn the crank a few times and add the beaten whites of 2 eggs. Freeze hard.

MISS BESSIE BEALL.

MILK SHERBET.

Strain juice of 6 lemons, add sugar enough to make as thick as batter, let stand an hour or so. Just before freezing add 3 pints of fresh milk, and freeze very slowly. Milk will look curdled, but will come out beautifully smooth and light, if turned very slowly.

MRS. ORVILLE D. PARKER.

PINEAPPLE SHERBET NO. 1.

Two and one-half pounds of sugar.

Three quarts of water.

One can of grated pineapple.

Juice of 1 lemon.

Whites of 8 eggs.

Boil the sugar $\frac{1}{3}$ to a syrup. Add a quart of water to the pineapple; then the lemon, and then the syrup.   When half frozen, add the whites of the eggs, beaten to a stiff froth.   Freeze.

San Angelo.   MRS. A. J. BAKER.

PINEAPPLE SHERBET NO. 2.

One pint can of grated pineapple, 1 pound of sugar, juice of 3 lemons, 1 quart of water.   Mix all together and strain through a cloth, pressing hard to get all the juice.   Whip the whites of 2 eggs; add to the juice, and freeze.

MISS EMMA CHAPMAN.

PINEAPPLE SHERBET NO. 3.

Four eggs (whites).
One and one-half pounds of white sugar.
One pint sweet milk.
Two quarts water.
One and one-half pounds pineapple (grated).
One and one-half teaspoonfuls lemon extract.
Five teaspoonfuls fruit acid.
Freeze.
Fruit acid: Four ounces citric acid, and 1 pint of water.

MRS. ANNIE P. NORTON.

SHERBET.

One-half box gelatine, dissolved in 1 pint cold water; then add 1 quart boiling water, juice of 4 lemons, 1 can grated pineapple sweetened to taste, whites of 3 eggs beaten stiff; put in a gallon freezer and if not full, fill up with clear water.   Freeze.

MRS. SAM HARLAN.

LEMON ICE.

One quart water, 4 lemons, 1½ pounds of sugar, whites of 2 eggs. Slice off the lemon rind and boil a few minutes; when cool add the juice of 4 lemons, and strain onto the beaten whites.   Freeze.

Victoria.   MRS. R. L. DABNEY.

ORANGE ICE.

Place on the fire 1 quart of water and 3 cups of sugar.   Chip the yellow rind from 3 oranges and 1 lemon, then add to the syrup; boil 5 minutes and stand away to cool.   Then add to it the juice of 6 large oranges and 3 lemons, and another quart of water; strain, freeze and pack.   This is delightful.

San Angelo.   MRS. A. J. BAKER.

10—C. B.

THE FAMOUS FRUIT PUNCH.

Press thoroughly 3 dozen lemons and 1 dozen oranges, 6 cans of sliced pineapple. Then pour over the rind of the lemons and oranges and pineapple pulp sufficient boiling water to cover. When cool, mix with the juices of the fruit (after straining) 1 quart of best cold tea, 3 cans of cherries, sugar to taste.

Plum preserves or jelly adds greatly to the fine flavor of the punch.

Plenty of ice.

If desired use fruit coloring or more lemon, if required, all depending on quality of lemons. I always slice very thinly 3 oranges and add also a few pieces of the pineapple and cherries.

MRS. BENEDETTE B. TOBIN.

ROMAN PUNCH.

Take a good watermelon and squeeze all the juice out; 3 quarts of juice, sweeten to taste; half a box of gelatine, cover with just enough water to soften and make a little gelatine, and when cold, add to the watermelon juice; freeze and serve in glasses.

MRS. LAURA McKEAN.

FROZEN FRUIT.

One 3-pound can of peaches.

One can grated pineapple.

Juice of 4 oranges.

One cup of sugar, or more if desired.

When in season, 1 box of strawberries is an agreeable addition.

Run the peaches through a colander, as lumps freeze hard; add the pineapple, orange juice, and sugar; put into 1-pound baking powder cans and pack in ice and salt for 3 hours, repacking once during this time. When ready to serve slip out of the cans, slice in inch slices across and serve with whipped cream and Marachino cherries.

MRS. RECTOR THOMSON.

MOOSE.

One pint of cream, whipped stiff with ½ pint sherry wine; sweeten to taste, then a cup of gelatine.

Put to freeze, alternating the cream with layers of chopped almonds and crystalized cherries.

MRS. GEORGE ASH.

ORANGE JELLY.

Juice of 2 oranges, rind of 1.

One lemon, juice and peel.

One package gelatine, dissolved in cold water.

One and one-half cups sugar.

One small cup of wine.

One good pinch of cinnamon.

Squeeze the juice into bowl with the grated peel and cinnamon. Pour on the boiling water, cover closely and let stand half an hour. Strain, and add sugar; let come to a boil; stir in gelatine and when this is dissolved, take the kettle from fire and strain through double flannel. Let stand till congealed.

Victoria.   MRS. R. L. DABNEY.

WINE JELLY.

To 1½ boxes of gelatine add 1 pint cold water, juice of 3 lemons, grated rind of 2; let stand 1 hour, then add 4 cupfuls loaf sugar, 3 pints of boiling water; boil 5 minutes; just before straining through flannel bag, stir in 1 pint sherry wine and 1 tablespoonful of brandy.

Serve with whipped cream.

                                             MRS. JOHN ORR.

NESSLERODE PUDDING.

Make a custard of 6 eggs and 6 tablespoons of sugar to 2 quarts of milk. When half frozen add 2 pounds of candied fruit, Maraschino, 1 pound of chopped almonds and 1 pint of whipped cream. Pack well and let stand, as it does not freeze easily.

                                        MRS. WALTER WILCOX.

FRUIT MOUSSE.

Whip a pint of cream very stiff; turn it into a sieve to drain. Mix with it a cupful of any fruit pulp (canned peaches will do nicely), the juice drained off and the pulp mixed with enough powdered sugar to make it of the same consistency as the whipped cream; a little "fruit coloring" makes it a pretty color; add 1 teaspoon of vanilla extract. Mold and pack in ice and salt for 3 hours. This can be put in 1-pound baking powder cans; put a piece of greased paper in top of can before putting on the tin top, then pack in salt and ice.

                                      MRS. EDWARD ROBINSON.

MOUSSE.

Whip a pint of cream very stiff; turn it onto a sieve to drain for a few minutes, so as it will be entirely dry. Return it to the bowl and whip into it lightly 4 tablespoonfuls of powdered sugar and a tablespoonful of curacao. When a liqueur is used for flavoring, less sugar is needed than with coffee, chocolate or essence. Turn the cream into a mold and pack it in ice and salt for 4 hours. Garnish the dish with small iced cakes.

MRS. A. S. WALKER.

AMBROSIA.

One can of pineapple.
One cocoanut, grated.
One dozen oranges, cut up rather fine.
Fill a glass dish with alternate layers of fruit and powdered sugar, with cocoanut on top. Use all the juice of the pineapple.

MRS. NORVAL WILSON.

NOTE.—This is delicious, but can be made very nice without the pineapple.—MRS. E. G. M.

ITALIAN CREAM.

Soak ⅓ box gelatine half an hour in cold milk.
Put a quart of milk on to boil, and when boiling, stir in yolks of 8 eggs, well beaten; add 1½ cups of sugar and the gelatine; when custard begins to thicken, take it off and pour into deep dish in which the 8 whites have been beaten stiff; mix well together, flavor with vanilla, put in molds; allow 4 hours to congeal.

MRS. LAURA MCKEAN.

BAVARIAN CREAM.

One pint cream, ½ box gelatine, ½ cup water, 1 pint milk, 2 ounces chocolate, ½ cup sugar, 1 teaspoon vanilla. Cover the gelatine with the water and soak half an hour. Whip the cream; grate the chocolate; put the milk on to boil, when boiling add the chocolate and gelatine, stir until dissolved, take from the fire, add the sugar and vanilla. Turn into a basin to cool. Stir continually until it thickens. Add the whipped cream; mix carefully. Turn into a mold to harden. Serve with whipped cream around the base.

MISS ELLA F. FULMORE.

WHIPPED CREAM.

Have cream sweet and cold as possible; whip in a cold flat dish with an egg beater till it begins to thicken, then add sugar to taste, and flavoring. Put in a cool place, or on ice if possible, till ready to serve.

CHARLOTTE RUSSE NO. 1.

One pint cream, put in a cold dish and whipped until stiff; add 1 teacup of white sugar, 2 teaspoons of vanilla extract, ½ wine glass of sherry wine; ¼ box Cox's gelatine, put into a tumbler, cover with hot water; when dissolved, add enough cold water to make the glass ¾ full; stir this into the whipped cream, put the gelatine in last; mix all together, put in bowl, and then put on ice.

MRS. EDWARD ROBINSON.

CHARLOTTE RUSSE NO. 2.

One ounce of gelatine dissolved in 2 gills of boiling milk.
Whites of 4 eggs, beaten to a stiff froth.
One and one-half cups of sugar.
One pint of thick cream, whipped very stiff.
Flavor to taste.
Mix the gelatine, sugar, cream and flavoring together; add lightly the whites of the eggs.
Line mold with thin slices of sponge cake or lady fingers dipped in Madeira or sherry wine; pour mixture over this, and put in ice box until required. This is a very simple and most delicious recipe.

BENEDETTE B. TOBIN.

BLANC-MANGE.

One quart milk.
One-half cup sugar.
Eight tablespoons corn starch or flour.
One-fourth teaspoon of salt.
Put milk to boil; moisten the starch and add to the milk, stir till it thickens; add sugar, salt and flavor to taste; pour in cups, put in a cool place to harden, serve with cream.

Victoria.   MRS. R. L. DABNEY.

CHOCOLATE BLANC-MANGE.

Half box gelatine, soaked till dissolved in as much cold water as will cover it; 1 quart of sweet milk, 1 cup of sugar, 2 blocks of sweet chocolate, grated; boil milk, sugar and chocolate 5 minutes; add gelatine, and boil 5 minutes more; flavor with vanilla, put in molds, and eat with whipped cream.

MRS. LAURA McKEAN.

BISQUE PUDDING.

Yolks of 4 eggs and $\frac{1}{2}$ cup sugar creamed; add lightly the beaten whites and 1 pint of whipped cream; then flavor. Pack in freezer and let stand 2 or 3 hours.

MISS LILLIE MELASKY.

SNOW CUSTARD.

Three eggs, 2 cups of sugar, $\frac{1}{2}$ package of gelatine, juice of 1 lemon. Soak the gelatine 1 hour in a teacup of water, add 1 pint of boiling water, stir until thoroughly dissolved; add $\frac{2}{3}$ of the sugar and lemon juice; beat the whites of the eggs very stiff, and when gelatine is cold whip it into the whites, a spoonful at a time. When finished put in glasses, previously wet with cold water. When congealed turn out in a saucer. Make a custard of $1\frac{1}{2}$ pints milk, yolks of the eggs and remainder of sugar; flavor with vanilla. Put several candied cherries on top of mold. Pour sauce around.

MRS. LAURA McKEAN.

Pickles, Sweet Pickles, Chow Chow and Catsup

Most of the members of the House of Representatives turned to face the cameras when they sat for their portrait in 1910. Note the strategically placed cuspidors in the center of the floor.

PICKLES, SWEET PICKLES, CHOW CHOW AND CATSUP.

CUCUMBER PICKLES.

Place small cucumbers in brine, strong enough to float an egg. Having been previously boiled and skimmed.

Let stand in this till you are ready to pickle. Then place in fresh water over night to freshen.

Scald in water in which there is a small piece of alum and some cabbage leaves.

Boil the vinegar with a little spice and sugar.

Wipe cucumbers dry, place in jars and cover with the hot vinegar.

MRS. SAM WEISIGER.

PICKLES—EXCELLENT.

Buy good firm barrel pickles, quarter, and pour on equal parts of vinegar and water enough to cover; add 1 or 2 pods of red pepper, and spice and sugar to taste. Heat to boiling point. It is then ready for use.

MRS. NORVAL WILSON.

CANTELOUPE PICKLES.

Take fine ripe canteloupes; pare and quarter them, cover with vinegar and let stand 24 hours. Then measure off the vinegar, leaving about 1 quart. To each quart add 3 pounds of brown sugar, cinnamon, cloves, mace and ginger to taste. Put vinegar and spice over the fire, when it boils drop in the fruit. Cook about 25 minutes, until it looks clear.

In 2 or 3 weeks it will be ready for use.

Victoria. MRS. R. L. DABNEY.

PEACH SWEET PICKLE.

Seven pounds peaches, 3 pounds good brown sugar, 1 quart vinegar, 1 teaspoon cinnamon, 1 of cloves, 1 of spice. Boil the sugar, vinegar and spices 15 minutes; then add peaches, and boil until tender. Next day pour off syrup and heat until boiling hot and pour over fruit. Repeat this three days, then tie up and set away.

Mrs. K. C. Estill.

WATERMELON RIND SWEET PICKLE.

Peel, trim and cut nicely in small pieces. Soak in cold water over night. Then in the morning put 2 pounds of rind to 1 pound of sugar, 1 pint of vinegar, spices, white ginger root, mace, cinnamon and cloves to taste; boil gently till tender and clear.

Mrs. R. L. Dabney.

PEACH OR PLUM SWEET PICKLE.

Three pounds of fruit, 1 pound sugar, 1 quart of vinegar, spice to taste. Boil sugar and vinegar together and put in fruit, and boil until thick enough to keep.

GREEN TOMATO PICKLE.

One peck of green tomatoes, sliced.

One dozen onions, sliced.

Sprinkle with salt, and let stand over night. Then drain and put into a vessel on the fire with vinegar, and let boil till tender; then add 1 cup of sugar, 1 teaspoonful of pepper, same of white mustard seed, ½ teaspoonful each of cinnamon, mace and allspice. Seal in jars.

Mrs. M. A. Chapman.

PICKLED STUFFED PEPPERS.

Twelve large green peppers; cut off the stem end of each, and save for cap; throw away the seed.

Filling: Chopped cabbage, red and black pepper, allspice, cloves, ginger, nutmeg and salt to taste.

Stuff the peppers with this, press cap on each pepper. Put in jars and cover with cold vinegar.

Tehuacana. Mrs. Kate Pearson.

GREEN TOMATO PICKLE.

One peck of green tomatoes, peeled and sliced thin.

Twelve onions, sliced thin.

Sprinkle with 1 pint of salt, and let stand over night. In the morning squeeze out of brine, and add 1 cup of brown sugar, 1 ounce each of black pepper, cloves, horse radish, tumeric, mustard seed, celery seed, 1 small bottle of prepared mustard. Mix well, put in bottles, place in a pan of cold water, set on stove, let heat well, pour on vinegar to cover, and seal.

MRS. GEO. WALLING.

CHOW CHOW (EXCELLENT).

One gallon green tomatoes.
One-half dozen peppers (green or ripe).
Two large onions.
One small head of cabbage.
One teaspoon of ground cloves.
One teaspoon of ground cinnamon.
One tablespoonful of mustard.
One cup of sugar.

Chop tomatoes and cabbage and sprinkle with ½ cup of salt; mix well; let stand over night. Next morning drain off the water; then add onions, peppers and seasoning, and run through a meat mill. Put in a granite vessel, cover with vinegar, and boil about 1 hour. Put in Mason jars, and seal.

Tehuacana. MRS. SUE E. VANNOY.

CHOW CHOW (SPLENDID).

One and one-half dozen barrel pickles, cut in small pieces.
Four large white heads of cabbage, chopped fine. Sprinkle with salt, let stand in sun or over night.
One dozen large white onions, 8 green peppers; cut fine, and soak in salt water.
Squeeze all out and place in kettle with following:
Two ounces white mustard seed.
One ounce of celery seed.
One pound of Coleman's English Mustard.
One and one-half pounds sugar.

After all is in the kettle, cover with vinegar (about 1 gallon) and let boil till it begins to thicken (from 1 to 2 hours), stirring constantly. When done let it cool some, and put up in jars; pour a little vinegar over each jar before sealing.

Waco. MRS. R. T. FLEWELLEN.

PICCALILLI.

Made of green tomatoes and onions.

One peck of tomatoes, sliced thin.

Eight large onions, sliced thin.

Place in separate vessels, sprinkle well with salt, and let stand over night. In the morning squeeze out and cook with a quart of vinegar, 1 pound of brown sugar, 1 teaspoon each of cloves, pepper and mustard.

MRS. G. CROW.

TOMATO CATSUP.

Wash and mash your tomatoes and boil them for half an hour, then strain them through a sieve, putting in the pulp. To 1 gallon of the liquid 1 quart of vinegar, 2 tablespoons of ground mustard, 2 tablespoons of pepper, 2 of salt, 2 tablespoons of allspice, 2 tablespoons of cloves, 2 or 3 onions cut fine, 8 pods of red pepper, and ½ teacup of sugar. Then boil to the proper consistency. Must have the best apple vinegar.

MRS. A. S. RUTHERFORD.

COLD TOMATO CATSUP.

One-half peck tomatoes, chopped fine.

Two roots of grated horse radish.

One teacup of salt.

One-half teacup of mixed white and black mustard.

Two teaspoonfuls of black pepper.

Two red peppers cut fine, leaving out the seed.

Two bunches of celery.

One cup of nasturtiums.

One cup of onions, cut fine.

One tablespoonful each of powdered cloves, mace, cinnamon.

One cup of sugar.

One quart of vinegar.

Cork tight, but do not seal.

MISS EMMA CHAPMAN.

CUCUMBER CATSUP.

Peel cucumbers, cut and slice, or chop fine.

Two chopped onions to 3 quarts of cucumbers. Place in a bowl, and sprinkle well with salt; let stand over night. Next morning drain off water, season with pepper, black mustard and a little celery seed. Fill in wide mouthed bottles, more than half full; then fill with good cider vinegar. Cork tight.

Victoria.   MRS. R. L. DABNEY.

TOMATO CATSUP.

To every gallon very red tomatoes, sliced (not peeled), add 5 tablespoons salt; 2 of cayenne pepper, ground; 2 of black pepper; 1 teaspoon each of ground mace, cinnamon and allspice; ½ teaspoon cloves; 2 large onions, sliced; 1 tumbler of brown sugar; 1 quart of good apple vinegar; 1 large tablespoon mustard. Put all together in preserving kettle, and cook gently till it thickens (2 to 4 hours on a moderate fire, according to quantity). Strain when cold, and bottle; dip corks in hot water.

Waco.   MRS. R. T. FLEWELLEN.

GOOD CHILI SAUCE.

Twelve large ripe tomatoes.

Two large peppers, chopped fine.

Two large onions.

Two cups of vinegar.

One tablespoonful of salt.

One cup of brown sugar.

One teaspoonful each of allspice, cloves, nutmeg and ginger.

Before cooking, run all through a meat chopper. Boil all together till thick.

Tehuacana.   MRS. KATE PEARSON.

CHILI SAUCE.

One peck ripe tomatoes, peeled and chopped.

One-half dozen green sweet peppers, chopped.

One-half dozen ripe (or red) sweet peppers, chopped.

One-half dozen onions, chopped.

One cup of sugar.

Two tablespoons salt.

One quart vinegar.

One-half of a small box of mustard.

One tablespoon cloves, allspice, cinnamon; the whole spices preferable. Cook until thick and well done; when well corked will keep a whole year. Is especially nice with fresh pork or sausage.

MRS. L. P. SIEKER.

Preserves,
Brandied Fruits,
Jellies and Jams,
Wine

The flood on the Colorado in June 1935 moved the river up Congress Avenue toward the Capitol. This was the last major flood of the Colorado River at Austin since future high water was controlled by the Highland Lakes dam system.

PRESERVES, BRANDIED FRUITS, JEL-
LIES AND JAMS, WINE.

PRESERVED PEACHES.

Take ½ pound sugar to 1 pound of fruit. Peel the fruit and cut in halves. Have ready a syrup of the sugar and just enough water to moisten well; let it boil a few minutes before putting in the peaches. Boil slowly till the fruit is thoroughly done, then take out and, if the syrup is still not thick enough, let boil till the proper consistency. Put up in hot jars, and seal at once.

FIG PRESERVES.

Wash the figs in a weak soda or lime water. Make a syrup of ¾ pound sugar to 1 pound of fruit, and enough water to wet the sugar. Let it boil a few minutes before putting in the figs. Cook till done and take out and let the syrup boil till consistency of honey. Seal while hot.

APPLE PRESERVES.

Peel, quarter and core apples (Pippins or Rhode Island Greenings); weigh equal quantities of fruit and sugar; add several oranges, in quarters (seedless) and some bits of mace; boil slowly until the fruit is clear, then remove it, and boil down the syrup to proper consistency. Place the fruit in jars, covering it with the syrup.

Mrs. J. B. Clark.

PEAR PRESERVES.

Cut the pears in halves; peel, and boil them in clear water until tender, which will take some time. Then make a syrup of sugar and water, allowing ¾ pound sugar to each pound of fruit, using as little water as possible; add sliced lemon to suit taste. When syrup is thick put in pears, and boil slowly till well done.

Mrs. Robert C. Shelley

STRAWBERRY PRESERVES.

Use large, firm berries; wash and pick.   One measure of berries to ¾ measure of sugar.   Make a syrup of sugar and enough water to dampen.   Let syrup boil almost to candy, put berries in carefully, boil slowly till proper consistency.

Mrs. E. G. Myers.

TOMATO PRESERVES.

Remove the skins from tomatoes by boiling for a few moments in clear water.   Take 1 pound of sugar to 1 pound of fruit, and thin slices of lemon, and let all stand together over night.   Pour off the juice and let boil, skimming well; then put in tomatoes and boil for half an hour; take out tomatoes on a dish, and let cool.   When syrup has thickened, put the tomatoes in jars, and pour over them the syrup.

WATERMELON RIND PRESERVES.

Soak the rinds three days in salt water; then in clear water until they are entirely fresh, changing it twice a day.   Then boil them in water until they look transparent; take out and soak them 24 hours in clear water.   Make a syrup of 1½ pounds of sugar to 1 pounds of rinds; put them in; stew them slowly until done.   Ice melons may be done in same way.   Be sure to peel them.

King and Queen Co. Va., 183— · Catharine F. Boulware.

From old recipes in possession of Mrs. J. B. Clark.

CITRON—GOOD.

Quick way to make.

Peel watermelon rind of 1 good sized melon very thin and carefully, then cut all of the red meat and the soft white of the rind, leaving green rind about ¼ inch thick.   Cut in fancy shapes and notch the edges.   Do this late in the evening; then put to soak over night in salt water, 1 teacup of salt and enough water to cover rind.   Next morning pour off salt water, and cover with fresh and let soak for 2 hours, then change water.   When it tastes fresh scald in alum water, ½ teaspoon alum to enough hot water to cover; in ½ hour take out of alum water, pour on fresh again and let soak till alum taste is out; then boil till tender in ginger tea, about 4 or 5 pieces of root ginger to 1 gallon of water.   Take out and weigh.   Make a thick syrup, allowing 1½ pounds sugar to 1 pound rind (if you have no scales convenient, measure the rinds and allow a heaping measure of sugar to a level one of rinds). Put just enough water in sugar to wet; then place on stove and add 2 sliced lemons and a small hand full of cinnamon and mace mixed; put in rinds and when syrup has cooked to consistency of honey take off and put up in air tight jars.

Mrs. J. K. Holland.

WATERMELON RIND PRESERVES.

Soak the rind over night in a gallon of cistern water in which 1 cup of lime has been dissolved. Then make a syrup, allowing a pound of sugar to each pound of rind. Slice several lemons, and preserve with it.

Miss Ella Bedell.

CANTELOUPE PRESERVES.

The melons should be ripe, sound and firm. Peel and cut them in pieces about an inch square; add sugar, ¾ pound to each pound of melon; sprinkle with alum water to keep it from boiling to pieces After standing over night, cook slowly until the melon is transparent, then dip out the melon and boil down the syrup to a proper thickness, adding to it when cool flavoring of orange extract.

Mrs. J. B. Clark.

BRANDIED PEACHES.

Pear peaches are best, but any nice large cling stone peach will do. Peel peaches, and weigh; to every 4 pounds of peaches and 2 pounds of sugar use 1 pint of good brandy. Take sugar with enough water to dissolve and boil until very thick; then drop in peaches, and boil 5 or 10 minutes, don't boil too tender; take the fruit out, boil syrup almost to candy, pour in brandy and remove immediately from the fire. Place peaches in jars and cover with syrup; seal air tight.

Mrs. Sam Harlan.

BRANDIED PEACHES.

Put the peaches in boiling water for a few minutes, when the skin will come off easily. Make a syrup of ½ pound sugar and ½ teacup of water for each pound of peaches. Skim well as the skum rises in boiling, then put in the peaches and boil till tender, no longer. Take them out carefully, fill your jars. Remove syrup from fire; add ½ pint of best brandy to every pound of peaches.

Mrs. J. D. Roberdeau.

Either of the above will answer for any fruit.

GENERAL RULES FOR JELLY.

Cover the fruit with water; let boil till water is well colored, strain and boil again for 15 minutes. Equal measures of sugar and fruit water. The smaller the quantity cooked together, the better it jellies; therefore, it is better to use several small vessels. Boil very rapidly; it should jelly in 15 or 20 minutes, but it is safer to try a little in a spoon before taking off. Put up hot in glasses, and cover.

All fruit jellies are made in this way.

CRAB APPLE JELLY.

Remove the blossom, and wash the fruit; put on to cook in cold water, and cover. When the fruit is done measure the juice, and to every pint use 1 pound of sugar; place the juice, uncovered, over the fire and boil 20 minutes, taking care that it boils steadily; after the juice is placed on the fire pour the sugar in a pan and put in oven to heat, if it browns slightly it will do no harm. When the 20 minutes are ended, turn the sugar into the liquid; let the whole come to a boil, and boil 3 minutes. Pour in glasses while boiling hot.

Mrs. E. P. Raynolds.

APPLE JELLY.

Take pippin apples, nicely prepared; stew and press the juice, and to each cup of juice add 1 cup of sugar. Flavor with cinnamon. Boil 10 minutes, or until it jellies.

Mrs. J. B. Clark.

BLACKBERRY JAM.

To each pound of berries add 1 of sugar. Crush the berries first; add sugar, and boil till thick and smooth, stirring constantly with a wooden spoon or paddle.

Mrs. J. D. Roberdeau.

DEWBERRY JAM.

Pick, wash and weigh your fruit; to every pound put 1 of sugar. Put fruit on fire alone, mashing it as it heats; allow it to boil 30 minutes, stirring almost constantly, crushing any berries that still may be whole; meanwhile place the sugar in oven in a pan, so it will be thoroughly heated at the end of 30 minutes; add sugar to fruit, and let boil 20 minutes longer; then put in jars while hot, and seal.

MRS. E. P. RAYNOLDS.

Berries of any kind may be done in the same way.

WINE.

One bushel of grapes, picked nicely; 10 quarts of water. Crush the grapes, add water and let stand 24 hours. Strain and put 2 pounds of sugar to a gallon of the grape water.

Victoria.   Recommended by MRS. R. L. DABNEY.

UNFERMENTED WINE.

One-half bushel mustang or domestic grapes; wash, pick and mash; put on with a gallon of water and boil until grapes are soft, then strain through colander, then strain 3 times through flour sack; sweeten to taste; just let it come to a boil, skim well, and seal while hot.

MRS. L. B. ESTES.

CANNED FRUITS AND VEGETABLES.

CANNED FRUITS.

Pears or peaches parboiled till tender; make a thick syrup and, after putting fruit in hot jars, pour over them the syrup.

Mrs. Geo. Walling.

CANNED GRAPES.

Use wild, green grapes, before the seeds harden. Wash and put in jars and cover with cold, clear water. Seal.

CANNED BERRIES.

Heat berries slowly to boiling point; then add 1 tablespoon of sugar to each quart of fruit; boil 15 minutes, and can. Mason jars answer the same purpose as cans.

CANNED TOMATOES AND OKRA.

Peel tomatoes and cook well; cut the okra in small pieces and add to the tomatoes; boil up. Put in Mason jars, and seal.

Mrs. Geo. Walling.

CANNING CORN.

Cut the corn from the cob and cook with water enough to keep it from burning. To every 6 quarts of corn allow 1 ounce of tartaric acid dissolved in boiling water. Seal like any other canned goods. To prepare for the table, pour off the sour water, saving it. Use fresh water to cook the corn, and to every quart of corn add $\frac{1}{2}$ teaspoon of soda. If the corn turns yellow there is too much soda, which must be neutralized by the tartaric acid water; pour in enough of that you turned off the corn at first to turn the corn white. While cooking add a spoonful of white sugar, and when nearly done, season with salt, pepper and butter.

Recommended by Mrs. Geo. Walling.

Confectionery

A stereoview of the Capitol, ca. 1936. By adjusting the distance of this picture from the eyes and focusing, some people are able to see this in three-dimension without using a stereopticon.

CONFECTIONERY.

SUGAR CANDY (TAFFY).

Two cups of sugar, ½ cup of water, 1 tablespoon of vinegar; cook till a little on a spoon will harden in cold water. Pour on a buttered dish, and when cool enough, butter the fingers and pull lightly, using only the finger tips to insure its being porous.

MOLASSES CANDY.

Boil 2 cups of molasses and 1 cup of sugar with a teaspoon of vinegar and a pinch of soda. Boil till it makes a hard wax; pour on buttered dish, and pull.

CHOCOLATE BUTTER SCOTCH.

Three cups sugar, 1 cup grated chocolate, 2 spoons butter, water to dissolve; boil till it ropes (not too hard). Pour in buttered pans.

MRS. E. G. MYERS.

CHOCOLATE CARAMEL.

One coffee cup of rich cream, 1 coffee cup brown sugar, 1 coffee cup molasses, butter size of an egg. Boil all together 20 minutes, then add 7 tablespoons of powdered chocolate, and boil until done. Pour into flat, buttered pans; cut into squares before it hardens.

MISS MARGARET CRISER.

PECAN CANDY.

One cup picked out pecans, 1 cup sugar. Put the sugar on the fire, stirring constantly until melted. Take off the fire at once, stir pecans in quickly and pour on buttered marble slab. Press out thin while hot.

MISS BESSIE BEALL.

SUGARED PECANS.

Fill a flat buttered dish with pecans. Make a syrup with 2 cups of sugar and enough water to dissolve. Cook till it ropes, then pour slowly on pecans, stirring contantly till it sugars.

MRS. E. G. MYERS.

PEANUT CANDY.

Two cups granulated sugar, 1 cup of chopped peanuts. Put sugar in hot frying pan and melt to a light brown (don't burn). When melted, stir in peanuts quickly and pour in buttered pans or roll thin on marble slab.

COCOANUT CANDY.

Grate 1 cocoanut. Make a syrup of 1½ pounds white sugar wet with water; cook until brittle. Beat whites of 2 eggs and add to them slowly the syrup; beat well and add cocoanut; beat until it whitens. Pour on a flat buttered dish, and cut in squares when cool.

STUFFED DATES.

Take seeds from nice firm dates; pick out pecans without breaking the meat, and put in the dates; press together, and roll in powdered sugar.

Another way is to use marshmallow in place of pecans.

MISS FRANK SMITH.

UNCOOKED FRENCH CANDY.

Break whites of 2 eggs into a bowl; add equal quantity of cold water, and stir in powdered sugar to make it stiff enough to be molded into shape; flavor to suit taste. This is the foundation for nearly all fancy candy.

A FEW FANCY CANDIES.

Make balls of the uncooked French candy, and press walnuts or pecans to each side. Or cut in squares, and put dates or raisins on each side. Or you can put in a little fruit coloring before forming into balls.

TABLE OF CONTENTS.

~~~~~~~~~~

COMPARATIVE WEIGHTS AND MEASURES.

Sixty drops make one teaspoonful.

Eight large tablespoonfuls make one gill.

One common sized tumbler holds one-half pint.

Ten eggs make one pound.

Two cups of butter equal one pound.

Two and one-half cups of sugar equal one pound.

Three and one-half cups of flour equal one pound; or

One quart of flour equals one pound.

INDEX TO ADVERTISEMENTS.